SELF DEFENCE

Syd Hoare started Judo at the age of fifteen and within eighteen months gained his Black belt – one of the youngest ever. He subsequently went on to compete in the Olympics and gain his 6th Dan (red and white belt). After three years in the Army, serving in Cyprus and Germany, he went to Japan where he stayed for nearly four years. During his time in Japan he trained in Judo, Karate, Aikido, Taichichuan, Bojitsu (stick-fighting), Taihojitsu (police arrest techniques) and Jujitsu. In addition to his interest in Eastern martial arts he has fenced, boxed and wrestled. Syd Hoare is also the author of *Teach Yourself Judo*.

TEACH YOURSELF BOOKS

SELF DEFENCE

Syd Hoare

TEACH YOURSELF BOOKS
Hodder and Stoughton

First printed 1982

Copyright © 1982
Syd Hoare
Illustrations copyright © 1982
Hodder and Stoughton Ltd

British Library Cataloguing in Publication Data

Hoare, Syd
Self defence.—(Teach yourself books)
1. Self-defence
I. Title
613.6'6   GVIIII

ISBN 0 340 26834 4

Printed and bound in Great Britain for
Hodder and Stoughton Educational,
a division of Hodder and Stoughton Ltd,
Mill Road, Dunton Green, Sevenoaks, Kent,
by Richard Clay (The Chaucer Press) Ltd,
Bungay, Suffolk. Photoset by
Rowland Phototypesetting Ltd,
Bury St Edmunds, Suffolk.

Contents

Introduction

Learning self defence is similar in some ways to insuring your house. The chances that your house will burn down are fairly remote, as are the chances that you will be violently assaulted. Yet most people insure their house, while surprisingly few will take out a personal insurance in the form of self-defence lessons. One difference between house insurance and violence against the person, however, is that the chances that your house will burn down remain relatively static, yet the chances that you will be violently assaulted are on the increase.

There are two ways to approach self defence. You can get some idea of what it is all about and practise just a few of the basic moves, or you can go into it in some depth and spend a lot of time practising in the same way that a martial artist would. This book caters for both approaches. Surprisingly, in the case of self defence a little knowledge is not necessarily a dangerous thing. If you can act with confidence and use the element of surprise, any of the techniques in this book can be overwhelmingly effective. Knowledge of the self-defence situation should convince you of the need for awareness. With knowledge and awareness you are two-thirds of the way there.

The techniques in this book are drawn from many sources. No single combat system is sufficient for self defence, but all have something particular to offer. In the main, the techniques are derived from karate, judo, Aikido, unarmed combat, and from British, American and Japanese police arrest techniques. There are also quite a few moves that the street fighter will be familiar with. These have been systematised to cover the whole defence situation.

It will be slightly difficult to learn the techniques alone, since all the moves presuppose an attacker. However, with a willing friend you are ready to start, and all that is required is a careful reading of the book so as to avoid injuries.

S.R.H.

I

About Self Defence

The need for self defence

Violence is on the increase. In the USA, comparative statistics gathered by the Federal Bureau of Investigation for the years 1973 and 1977 showed an increase in aggravated assault of 24.2 per cent, robbery 5.4 per cent and rape 22.6 per cent. Statistics for England and Wales over the ten-year period 1969 to 1978 show an average annual increase of 9½ per cent in indictable offences of violence against the person, with a staggering 22 per cent increase in reported cases of rape in 1977–8. This latter may reflect a greater willingness to report such offences to the police (encouraged by greater anonymity afforded the victims by the courts), but is in accordance with the general trend: in England and Wales, as in the USA, there has been little change in the incidence of serious crimes such as murder, but a dramatic increase in 'less serious' offences involving violence or the threat of violence.

There seem to be no signs of any reversal in the continual annual increase in such crimes. All in all, the statistical picture is not one to encourage you to lower your guard. Some form of self-defence ability is becoming more and more necessary.

Not only is self defence useful for protecting yourself; it is of course useful for protecting your friends and family, the weaker members of society and the underdog. Once upon a time cries for help late at night were quickly answered. Nowadays it is possible in some parts of the world for a woman to be raped in daylight in a public place and to have her cries for help totally ignored. If more people became adept at self defence and were prepared to help the weaker members of society, violence at this level would surely decrease.

An ability in self defence can also have an effect on a person's personality. When you are not physically afraid of other people you are more likely to stick up for your rights and assert yourself where you should. In other words, the ability will make you more self-confident. In turn, potential troublemakers will avoid you when they sense your self-confidence.

In short, self defence is necessary to protect yourself and others, decrease the general level of violence, and increase your self-confidence.

Those who need self defence

Anyone may meet violence at some time or other, but there are readily discernible categories of people who may need self-defence capability more than others.

The most obvious group comprises the physically weaker members of society. This includes women, the elderly and children. Women are likely to meet violence in the form of rape and muggings. The elderly are also a target for muggers, and young children may suffer from bullying at the hands of older children.

The next group who need self-defence ability include those whose work it is to protect and defend. They include police, security forces and night guards.

Finally there is the man in the street. He may need to protect his family, friends and, occasionally, himself.

Depending upon the group in which you fall, your approach to self defence will be different. The different approaches will be explained later, but first you will need to know where you stand in the eyes of the law and something about the self-defence situation.

The law and self defence

You have the legal right to defend yourself, family and property, but the actions you take must be appropriate to the situation: you must not take a sledgehammer to crack a nut. The law expects you to avoid violence wherever possible; and where it is possible for you to run away, that is what the law expects you to do, even if it means swallowing your pride and losing face. When you are *forced* to defend yourself, family or property, you are expected to use the *minimum* degree of force in return. If you injure someone when defending yourself you may well be prosecuted if the law thinks you over-reacted.

In the UK you are *not* allowed to carry a weapon to defend yourself: if you do so you will be prosecuted for carrying an offensive weapon.

The expert boxer or karate man who gets in a fight and injures the other party will be more severely judged than the average citizen. You may feel it reasonable to learn to protect yourself, but it is as well to realise that the law may think otherwise.

Violence

There are various theories as to the causes of violence. Some claim that it has an evolutionary value in that it is (or was) necessary for the maintenance of food supply and procreation, i.e. the protection of job and family. Others say that man has a carnivorous nature and may enjoy seeing others suffer. Violence – especially ritualised fighting (which a lot of fighting is) – may be the arena for the demonstration of masculine bravery. Put another way, it may stem from the promotion or defence of an individual's self-image or reputation. Another theory proposes that there are three sub-cultural solutions that result in violence: the first is the conflict sub-culture composed of those who fail to meet society's ideals and who fight against them; the second is the criminal sub-culture in which violence is part of business and is impersonal and passionless; the third is the retreatist sub-culture, represented by drug addicts and various drop-outs. Apart from the criminal types, members of these sub-cultures appear to strike at society for rejecting them as failures.

Economic pressures and crowding may lead to the inability to cope with stress, which in turn leads to family violence, minor vandalism and aggravations. When people are under pressure, small incidents can easily touch off violence.

Most psychologists agree that violence is rarely random. That is to say, it usually fits into the violent person's background and culture, and has a cause. The victim, however, may feel that it is totally random.

Knowing some of the possible causes of violence may help in avoiding it. Obviously, a direct threat against a person's livelihood, his mate or family will touch off some very basic instincts, and is only made at your peril. Where you see someone demonstrating his bravery or protecting or enhancing his self-image you may well back down when it affects you: it is hardly worth getting hurt for such a trivial cause. When a criminal is at work, you must weigh up the pros and cons of action and act accordingly. When a person tries to injure you as a representative of a society which he thinks rejects him, try reasoning with him. His rejection of society may well have a rational basis. Against the person who inflicts injury because he enjoys seeing suffering, you can pretend to suffer, show no signs at all, or fight back, according to the situation.

These are mostly non-physical strategies for avoiding violence. Where possible, use your brains rather than your brawn. A story is told of a Japanese warrior who was an expert swordsman. One day he was challenged to a duel by a young, obviously inexperienced warrior, out to prove himself. He declined to fight several times but the young warrior pressed him and became more abusive. 'All right,' he said, 'let us not fight here, it is too crowded, let's go over to that small island and fight.' He rowed the abusive young man over to the island, held the boat steady for him to disembark, then, just as he was himself about to disembark, he suddenly pushed the boat away from the island and rowed back, leaving a furious – but still alive – young warrior behind him.

There may come a time when you are suddenly assaulted. This will leave you no time to reason or use the other non-physical means of avoiding violence. Then you must defend yourself as best you can. Attacks by the mentally deranged, drunks and drug addicts may be quite irrational and must be dealt with immediately.

Many of course will not be prepared to avoid violence by non-physical means: they will not back down, lose face, be robbed, or whatever. If they decide to defend themselves they must accept the possibility of being hurt, because self defence is not about certainties, it is about probabilities. If you know what to do about a knife thrust to the stomach it is not *certain* that you will stop it or avoid it – the best boxer in the world cannot avoid being punched in the face sometimes – but you increase your chances of stopping it, and the more proficient you get the greater are your chances. If someone wants your purse which has just a small amount of cash in it, you must decide whether to suffer the indignity and loss of money if you just hand it over, or a possible punch in the nose if you try to hang on to it. The final decision is up to you.

One Christian way to minimise any humiliation in backing down from a physical confrontation is to 'turn the other cheek'. Humiliation stems from being made to do what you do not want to do and your consequent feeling of loss of personal sovereignty. If someone wants to demonstrate his bravery let him do it and then give him the chance to demonstrate even more. If you turn the other cheek you are the master of the situation, not him.

The few studies of violence which have been made show that the more violent sex is the male, especially younger men. Violence tends to happen more in the summer, at night rather than by day, with Saturday night between 8 pm and 2 am as the peak time. Most violence occurs in the streets. Violence thus tends to occur during socialising hours and in social places, with drink and disputes over women as prominent features. So much is common wisdom. However, it helps to identify when and where we must be especially careful.

As to the type of injury, one survey of 636 fights in British public houses showed that 75 per cent of the resulting injuries were to the head and face. The injuries in order of frequency were: broken nose, broken teeth, black eye, concussion. This seems to indicate that in a social setting you are most likely to be struck in the face by a fist. Where there is a motive such as rape or robbery the assailant will attempt to control the victim, first by threat and then physically, either by catching hold or striking.

Conventions with regard to violence change. For many years in the English-speaking world kicking was frowned upon and differences were settled with the fists. However, the world-wide spread of oriental martial arts has led to the use and acceptance of kicking. Even so, it seems that it is the assailant's fists that you have to take special care of. One anthropologist's study of fighting all over the world showed a more or less uniform pattern. First there is a sudden explosion with one or both sides flailing into the other, arms swinging down and round, slapping rather than punching. Often this is followed by both falling to the ground and rolling around. The action tends to stop almost immediately when one side backs down. Certainly, such fights are totally unlike the fights of film and stage, and most people's image of a fight. In other parts of the world the use of the knife and hand-gun is much more common. Where such attacks are the norm you must learn to handle a knife and a gun yourself. This is outside the scope of this book, although some defences are given against them.

Self-defence technique

Most self-defence books are based on one combat form or another: the karate man writes a book which is mostly about karate defences; the judo man writes a book which is mostly about judo defences, and so on. A look at the self-defence situation soon shows that it is not possible to rely on one system alone, firstly because the various self-defence situations demand various types of technique, and secondly because in any one situation you may wish to achieve different ends.

When attacked, you can *avoid*, *control* or *incapacitate* the assailant. If someone rushes at you, you can stick a foot out, stumble him to the floor and then run away. Here you avoid violence, and the assailant is otherwise uninjured. Similarly, you can catch the assailant in a wrist-twist and hold him totally immobile. In this situation the assailant is controlled and not injured (the assailant only hurts himself if he struggles against the hold), and such techniques are therefore most used by policemen. If a lunatic swinging an axe rushes at you, you may knock him out with a blow to a sensitive spot. Here the assailant is incapacitated.

Avoidance techniques require a certain amount of physical dexterity, but are otherwise not difficult to learn. Techniques of control and incapacitation require speed, accuracy and power and take longer to master. The three categories also reflect an escalation of the amount of violence you may offer an assailant in return.

The techniques of self defence are drawn from the various systems of combat. Combat can be divided into two main categories: *striking* and *grappling*. In other words you either seek to hit the opponent or catch hold of him. Techniques of striking include punching, kicking, butting and jabbing with different parts of the body. Representatives of this type of combat are karate, boxing, Kung Fu, Tae-kwon-do and Savate. In the case of grappling techniques, the assailant is caught hold of and either thrown down, strangled, joint-locked or immobilised. Representatives of this type of combat are judo, wrestling, Aikido and Sanbo. Sometimes the combat systems overlap: judo includes some striking techniques and karate includes some throws.

The various types of combat technique applied to the self-defence situation have different functions.

Striking techniques are used mainly for incapacitation. An expert may be able to hit someone softly enough to make him change his mind about attacking or to keep him at bay, but a beginner may find that a soft punch is totally ineffective and will only escalate the violence. You usually have to make your blows count.

Throwing techniques are for avoidance or incapacitation, not control. An expert can throw hard enough to knock an assailant out, but for the non-expert the most likely result is to spill the assailant over, giving a chance to avoid the confrontation. A thrown assailant, however, does offer further opportunities for control or incapacitation with ground fighting techniques.

Strangling is purely an incapacitation technique. In a one-to-one situation, it is probably the most effective way of dealing with an assailant. A really tough assailant may be able to absorb a considerable amount of punishment from kicks and blows, but a strangle clamped on takes no more than about eight seconds to render him unconscious. *It also kills.*

Joint-locks control or incapacitate the assailant. Usually they are used for controlling, but if wrenched on hard enough will put him out of action. Some joint-locks such as spine- and neck-locks can be lethal.

One unquantifiable aspect of self defence is the *result* that the techniques will have on an assailant. A light punch to the nose, a controlling wrist-lock, or being turned upside down by a throw may literally knock the fight out of somebody even though he suffers very little pain. A short sharp shock, a sudden feeling of uncertainty or inferiority may do the trick. On the other hand they may really infuriate the assailant, causing him to attack even more ferociously. The victim of an assault is the only one to judge how to defend himself. Close observation of the assailant is of paramount importance at all stages of the confrontation: if it looks as though he has changed his mind, leave well alone.

The various types of technique are useful at different stages of a confrontation. Striking techniques are mostly appropriate if the assailant is at a slight distance from you. If you are leaped on or caught hold of, throws or arm-locks will probably be your most useful defence. If knocked to the ground with the assailant on top, judo techniques of strangling and arm-locking will be most effective. To be effective in self defence you have to learn to function at all stages of the confrontation, since it is not you who decides whether you are going to be grappled or struck. You must also learn to vary the type of technique you use in return, according to whether you want to avoid, control or incapacitate the assailant.

For those who have self defence in mind but want to practise the martial arts, I recommend combining one of the grappling arts, such as judo, with one of the striking arts, such as karate. The karate and judo combination will cover the effective use of fists and feet plus the ability to throw, strangle and joint-lock, and fight on the ground. Practising a martial art will make you fit, co-ordinated, courageous and used to handling bodies.

There are three aspects of self-defence ability: *knowledge* of the situation, *awareness*, and the actual physical *ability* to deal with an attack. With knowledge of the self-defence situation you will know that going home alone late on Saturday night, for example, is potentially dangerous. This should lead you, if the situation is unavoidable, to wear sensible shoes and clothing so that if necessary you can run or fight. Above all it should make you keenly aware of your surroundings. Keen awareness is of the highest importance: if you can see what is coming you can avoid it. In a potentially dangerous situation you must be constantly aware of all that is going on around you and be thinking ahead. This requires practice. It is no good relegating the importance of awareness to a slot in the back of your mind and hoping that you will be aware when the time comes. You probably won't be. If you are out at night, walking down the street or getting into your car, get into the habit of looking around you and checking what is going on. The first time you try this you will realise how unaware you usually are, since you will be doing something you do not usually do. With a little practice you will learn to keep your wits about you without becoming paranoid about it.

The importance of awareness is illustrated by the following story which took place during a long period of civil war in medieval Japan. Total cunning and treachery was the order of the day. Nobody was safe and everybody was suspect. Small groups of warriors would band together for protection. When not actually in combat they made it a rule, as part of their awareness training, to try to catch each other out at any time or in any place. Surprise attacks would take place in the middle of the night, in or around their headquarters or when they were bathing, eating or using the lavatory. In this way they became extremely difficult to take by surprise. It is reputed that one old warrior never slept properly in twenty years. Instead he sat lightly dozing propped up by his sword.

The toughest, most ferocious and skilful fighter can be beaten if he is day-dreaming or not paying attention. You should be aware at all times of who is behind you or what may lie round the next corner or dark doorway. By being aware you can take appropriate action. If someone is close behind you, do something about it. Never hope for the best or feel embarrassed about your counter-measures. With practice your manoeuvres can be made to look quite natural and not the actions of someone suffering from a persecution complex. Become aware, evaluate the situation, then *act*.

With some idea of the self-defence situation, and awareness, you will have already gained some measure of self-defence ability. The next stage is to practise the actual techniques.

2

General Principles of Self Defence

Situation evaluation

If you feel that trouble is brewing, the first thing you should do is evaluate the situation. Look carefully at your potential assailant. Is he wearing heavy boots which would be dangerous if he kicked at you? Is he wearing items of clothing you could catch hold of, such as tie, jacket or belt? Is his hair long enough to get hold of? If he is reaching into a pocket, is it likely that he is going for a knife? Is he edging nearer? What is he holding? All these questions should flash through your mind. Next, look to see if he has any friends nearby. As you look around also note your surroundings. Are there any handy objects that you could use to defend yourself with, such as a chair or a stick? Is there anything you could throw at your assailant, such as stones or dirt? Next, look at the general terrain. Is there anywhere you could position yourself which would be to your advantage, such as stairs, an entrance to a narrow alley, or higher ground? Is your footing sure, or is there somewhere where the assailant would find it difficult to move safely? Is the sun in your eyes or his?

Obviously you will not want, or perhaps be unable, to spend too long evaluating the situation, but the two or three seconds you spend will be of *enormous* advantage to you. Just briefly check:

1 the assailant;
2 friends and weapons (yours and his);
3 the general terrain;

then act quickly.

Keeping cool

You will not be able to function properly if you are terrified – or even just nervous. Like a mouse hypnotised by a swaying cobra, some people freeze in the face of violence. Violence can be an all-systems breakdown for you. Your mental and physical reactions must be rigorously controlled: you must keep cool. There is an intimate connection between the state of your mind, your breathing and your body position. Fear will make you flinch or even grovel. Your hunched position will affect your breathing, which will become shallow and uneven, and your mind will buzz like a disturbed bees' nest.

Reverse the whole process! Stand straight and square and give your rib-cage freedom to move. Take long, deep breaths. You should now be sufficiently composed to evaluate the situation.

Focus

If you are deeply interested in something, such as a beautiful view, you will look at it intently without any sense of strain. Conversely, you will not want to look at anything that repels you. Violence is a repellent situation and you will find yourself wanting to avoid looking at it. For your own safety, however, you must – and very intently.

Faced with a violent man the problem arises as to what part of him to look at. Should you watch his hands, or his eyes, or what? The answer is not to focus or stare at any one point, such as the hands, since you may miss the foot that is about to swing up. If you are beyond striking distance, gaze generally at the assailant's eyes but be peripherally aware of his feet and hands. If much closer, gaze generally about chest height but be peripherally aware of eyes, hands and feet. Try not to get misled by any particular movements of the hands. These may be a camouflage for some other attack. Most people cannot attack cold. They usually need to make some sort of minor preparatory move, such as a feint, before the main move.

With careful observation it is usually easy to see trouble coming. Many street fighters try to attack very unexpectedly. The time between the incident which sparks off the situation and the assault may be very short. For example, you may bump into someone in a bar. They then turn around, approach and hit you in the face. The approach, though brief, if often very casual. In this sort of situation be aware of the fact that street fighters erupt into violence very quickly, and be aware of any apparently casual movement in your direction. It is extremely difficult to make a really casual camouflage movement. If you watch carefully you will feel that something is wrong, and this should put you on your guard.

Fighting distance

When you are forced to defend yourself, the best distance to have between the assailant and yourself is one where you can hit him but he cannot hit you. This is not theoretically possible unless you have exceptionally long arms or legs. Usually it will be the same for both attacker and victim. However, what this refers to is the need to be in control of the space just a few inches beyond your reach and the attacker's reach.

If you are just out of reach you are safe, but in a position to launch a counter-attack. If you are too far away you will be unable to make any retaliatory move. As an attacker advances or retreats you must maintain your position just beyond his reach but be instantly ready to move in with a counter-attack. Appreciation of this fighting distance is vital in such combat arts as boxing and fencing.

If an attacker advances on you, do not necessarily back away. Instead, move round to your left or right. Backing away may be interpreted as fear.

Unfortunately the distance at which strangers talk to you is nearly always within striking distance. If a stranger approaches you in the street, perhaps to ask for directions, do not let him come too close. Instead, step back and reply and, if necessary, adopt the Social Stance (see page 20). Do not worry about being anti-social.

On many occasions, especially on social occasions and in crowded public places, you will not be able to maintain a safe distance. Sometimes you simply have to take people on trust. If you do feel there is any danger, take care to protect your back by standing, if necessary, against a wall. If this is not possible, always try to be aware of what is going on behind you.

Maintaining the initiative

If suddenly attacked, you will defend yourself as best you can. If, however, you have kept your wits about you and have seen trouble coming, you have a certain amount of scope in dictating how, when and where the confrontation will take place. The timing of your defensive moves in an attack is crucial in maintaining the initiative. You must always try to be one step ahead of the assailant.

There are roughly four phases to a confrontation:

1 The attacker *decides* to attack;
2 The attacker *prepares* to attack;
3 The attacker *attacks*;
4 The attacker *misses* (with your help).

With an attack that has a particular motive, such as rape or robbery, the decision to attack will have already been made, and the victim will not necessarily be aware of this phase. On many occasions, when the violence takes place more or less spontaneously, the victim will be aware of it. Initiating your defensive moves at phases one and two of the confrontation will enable you to maintain the initiative.

Deciding that the attacker has made up his mind to attack is a matter of fine judgment. Signs to look for are rapid eye movements, facial tension and pallor, unnatural stillness, clenching of fists and the general feeling that he is working himself up to do something.

Preparation for the attack may be indicated by foot movement as he eases himself into striking distance, and by hand movement as he lifts his arms in preparation to strike, catch hold, or go for a weapon. Some sort of diversionary feint may occur at this stage.

When you see these signs and you have judged that an attack is imminent, whip in suddenly with your own attack. How you attack is up to you. It will depend on what is your best offensive move. If you have developed a good punch or kick then use it. It is a matter of semantics as to whether this is attack or defence. Whatever it may be called, it will be necessary for you to be able to move offensively as well as defensively. This is why there are several offensive moves included in this book. Attack is the best form of defence.

The reason that phases one and two are good moments to counter-attack is because the attacker is mentally preoccupied with his own plans. He is not then solely concerned with what you are doing, but with what he is about to do.

Phase three, the attack in mid-flight, is the worst moment to deal with an attack unless you are an expert. If an assailant rushes at you swinging a punch at your jaw and you slip it (see page 26) prodding straight back at his face, the counter-blow will be extremely heavy, combining his impetus and the power of your body. If you are not an expert and try to stop such an attack dead with a kick or a punch you will probably get hurt. Action at this phase should be evasive action, such as a side-step or a parry, followed up by your main move when the attacker has missed. If skilfully done, the assailant may pitch off balance and crash to the floor with very little expenditure of energy on your part.

Thus the best times to deal with violence are the very early stages and end, not midway.

When you have dealt with the violence, there is a final phase where special care is needed. The assailant may be only momentarily subdued or be foxing, so when the situation has been contained stay just beyond fighting distance and watch the assailant. As the Zulu saying goes, 'When you have defeated the enemy, sharpen your spear'.

It is of enormous advantage to be able to evaluate the situation accurately and react as swiftly as possible. The second you see danger, move hard and fast either in to the attack or away. If you look at it from an assailant's point of view, his victim is an unknown quantity whom he must gain control of as early as possible. At the very beginning of a confrontation the options for the victim are wide open, but decrease rapidly as the situation develops. What the victim must not do is to stop to think for too long. He will probably think himself out of action:

> 'And thus the native hue of resolution,
> is sicklied o'er with the pale cast of thought'.

Most military combat training is based on the principle of swift reaction. Moves are often crude but succeed because the soldier hits first and asks questions later. In military combat, of course, there are fewer legal and social constraints. With ordinary street and city violence it is not suggested that you hit first and ask questions later – simply think quickly and act fast.

Mental control

The ultimate in self defence is to control an assailant mentally. However, mental control is a two-way thing: before you can control the assailant mentally, you must control yourself.

When you are nervous, uncertain, disgusted or abusive, the

assailant can read you like a book. As mentioned earlier, your own mental control springs from your posture and breathing. Stand square and regulate your in- and out-breathing, taking each breath down to below your navel. When you speak to the assailant, speak from your abdomen. Uncertainty will be reflected in a squeaky voice, whereas a deep firm voice will reflect control and strength. As you speak, control your nervousness but also eliminate any emotion such as disgust or pity from your voice. Simply speak neutrally.

As you talk to the potential assailant be aware of his eyes, as they often reflect his intentions, and also be aware of his breathing. His state of mind can be gauged from the disorder of his breathing. Most actions follow an in-breath, which can help you to judge when an attack may take place. Conversely the best time to handle an assailant is on his out-breath. As your eyes may reflect your intentions keep them steady and slightly narrowed. Through your eyes, breathing and voice try to harmonise with, and control, the mind of the assailant.

With your self under control in this way, avoid over-control of the assailant. Save his face and avoid challenges or threats, either his or yours. Remember that a fist or a raised arm is a threat, so maintain a Natural Stance as long as possible. Talk to the assailant all the time and try to elicit co-operation. Know how you want the situation to end and work towards it by letting the assailant know what you want. Try to achieve a rational solution of the situation. Try to avoid touching the assailant, but, if you have to, make it a very light touch.

Hopefully, through these means you can avoid a physical confrontation.

Armed assailant

An armed attacker has a huge advantage which must not be underestimated. A knife or a gun which is carried for actual use *will* be used without much ado. You must deal with it as best you can. When a weapon is used as a *threat* you have a greater chance to deal with it. Great care must be taken that you do not provoke the use of the weapon. Often a weapon is carried because it makes the owner feel tough. In such a situation relax and back down, and the weapon may then be put away. If it has to be dealt with, try to even up the odds by grabbing anything that can be used defensively or offensively, such as a chair or a stick (more for knife attacks). There is nearly always something to hand which can be thrown, or wielded. When facing an armed assailant the general rules are:

1 Show no resistance at all.
2 Talk and look for opportunities to act.
3 Deal with the weapon before the man.
4 Move out of the line of fire as you act.

Multiple assailants

Japanese Samurai films and Chinese Kung Fu movies abound with scenes of one man taking on anything up to fifty assailants. This, unfortunately, creats the myth that one man can easily handle more than one opponent. In most cases he cannot. Two men working together can easily overcome one man, especially if they come from different directions at the same time. If at all possible, therefore, avoid confrontation with more than one assailant; the odds are too great. Also do not imagine that you can handle such a situation by dealing with one of a group. Group members tend to identify with each other, even if there is in fact no particular binding common interest, and react together. There is an easily arousable dog-pack mentality.

If you have to face more than one assailant try to make your stand where they can only come at you one at a time, such as an alley-way or doorway. Also look for any weapon. If in the open, deal abruptly with single assailants, taking them out of action if possible. Swift action against the leader of the pack *may* help the others to change their minds. Try to shed as many superfluous clothes as possible. Make it as difficult as possible for them to catch hold of you. Protect your knuckles by wrapping something round them and look for something small, solid and heavy to hold which will make your punches heavier. As you defend yourself, constantly change position by zig-zagging, ducking, spinning and weaving. Try to crash the assailants into each other. At all costs do not fall to the ground. Be wary of groups of teenagers or even younger children. There is a tendency not to see the wood for the trees. One boy is no threat to an adult, but half a dozen or more certainly are: their combined weight can easily overwhelm you, as can a barrage of kicks and punches. Try to avoid groups like this, especially since you may be reluctant to hit youngsters. If you are jumped on you will have to defend yourself as best you can. However, if you can position yourself where you can handle them one at a time you should be fairly safe.

House and car

Part of self defence consists of taking reasonable precautions with your environment. Whether you are in it or not, your house needs to be secure against intruders. Windows and doors should have secure locks. Extra precautions need to be taken with the front door. A spy-hole is a useful device for checking callers without their necessarily being aware that you are in. If you then need to talk to them, a strong chain on the door which allows it to open a few inches is necessary. The actual door and its lock should be strong. Many front doors are so flimsy that a single strong kick can smash them open. If in doubt about the security of your home call in a reputable company which specialises in house security, or check with the crime prevention unit of your local police station.

Inside the house lockable internal doors are useful. If an intruder does manage to enter your house during the night he will have more obstacles to break through and you will have more chance of hearing him. Not only can you barricade yourself behind a door, but also the ability to lock doors behind you may give you time to escape from the house altogether.

A noisy dog is very useful in a house or flat. A dog will function as your second pair of (very keen) ears and, if it is big and ferocious enough, as your bodyguard as well.

If you live alone, some form of communication system with a neighbour is very useful. An alarm system with strategically placed buttons can easily be installed and connected to your nearest co-operative neighbour.

Outside the house you will need good lighting. Avoid any pools of darkness around your house or near the doors. Also take care to make your garage secure and well-lit.

When you are about to use your car, especially at night, look around before you fiddle with the car-keys. Also check that there is nobody already in the back seat. When you are in it make sure that all the doors are locked. Do not stop for hitch-hikers or for a car (other than a police car!) flashing its lights from behind. When parking the car, do so in a well-lit area.

3

Applied Self Defence

Basic technique

If you are flinching or cowering with fear you are not ready for action.
Your first move is to adopt a stance. Your stance has three functions.
Firstly, it affects your breathing and consequently your mental
control (see page 11). Secondly, it is the first positive move you will
make in a violent situation. It shows that you have accepted the
possibility of violence. Thirdly, it puts you in the best position to
attack or counter-attack. A stance may also have the added advantage
of deterring a would-be attacker. He may conclude that you know
what you are doing.

Many people refuse to believe that violence will be used against
them; consequently, when it does, they are caught wrong-footed.
Adopting a simple stance such as the Natural Stance will avoid this
mistake.

A very obvious fighting stance, such as that of a boxer or karate
man, has the disadvantage of showing both that you are ready and the
type of move you are likely to make. One way round this is to adopt the
neutral Natural Stance.

Natural Stance

Stand straight, feet about shoulder-width apart, with arms hanging
loosely by your side. You may either stand square on to your assailant,
or more side-on. Standing side-on has the advantage of reducing any
target you may offer. The Natural Stance is a neutral stance. The
assailant cannot tell at a glance that you are particularly ready, or how
you may move in defence. Keep your head up, control your breathing

and relax. Keep your assailant constantly in view (see Focus, page 11). From this stance you can move swiftly into action or you can use it as a preliminary position for the Ready Stance (see below). Even if you are doubtful as to whether violence will actually occur, get into the habit of adopting this position (Fig. 1).

Fig. 1

Ready Stance

With this stance you are more ready for action. Your open hands are up and in position for parrying, blocking, striking or catching hold. Stand with your left foot and side forward. Take most of your weight on your forward left foot. Your right foot is placed back about shoulder-width away with the weight on the *ball* of the foot, heel raised. Lift your arms up and position your hands at about shoulder height, left one forward, right one back. The fingers and thumb of each hand should be lightly touching each other (Fig. 2). This stance with the left side leading is for right-handed people. The left arm is used for parrying, blocking and light striking and the right arm packs the power punch. You may have to use either side, so practise moving smoothly into either position, taking care to keep the heel of the rear foot raised. For movement in the Ready Stance, see Movement (below).

Fig. 2

Social Stance

In a social situation, when you are in some doubt as to whether violence will occur, you may not want to adopt the Ready Stance for fear of looking ridiculous, or alarming an innocent person. In this case it is possible to adopt the fairly innocuous Social Stance, which is nevertheless effective. Stand almost sideways-on to your potential assailant, feet shoulder-width apart, left side forwards. Lift up your left hand and position it as if you were scratching your earlobe, grasping your chin or rubbing your cheek – the exact position does not matter so long as it looks natural. Place your right hand on your right hip. If you are sufficiently sideways-on, your right hand may be out of sight, in which case you may clench it.

In this stance your left hand is in position to intercept most blows to the upper body or make a swift blow itself. The right hand is also ready. This position can be held quite naturally for some time (Fig. 3).

Fig. 3

Movement

In everyday life one does not pay a lot of attention to how one moves around. Roads and paths are flat or well lit. In a self-defence situation, however, how you move may be of crucial importance. When you are under stress and concentrating on an assailant, movement around a dark room, on rough ground or in a rubbish-strewn area may be very difficult. There is a great danger that you may stumble or fall over, giving the assailant a good opportunity to attack.

In such circumstances the way to move is cautiously by *half-step*. You will naturally make this step when moving sideways: one foot moves out to the side and the other moves up close to it (ankle bone to ankle bone) without crossing over, and so on. This type of move applies when moving forwards or backwards. Move one foot forward and then bring the other foot up to within 12 inches of it, then advance the other foot again and so on. Try practising this movement in a pitch dark room and you will appreciate the importance of it. When you meet an obstruction you can quite easily stop without falling over.

Falling

It is not at all unlikely that you will get knocked over when defending yourself. When you do fall over you will need to minimise the shock of falling, especially if it is on a hard surface, and need to recover your position as quickly as possible. It is of vital importance to stay off the ground unless you know what to do there.

When falling backwards, practise the *judo fall*. As you go backwards bring your chin down on to your chest, relax, curve your body and roll backwards (Fig. 4). Keep the arms out of the way at the side of your body. Tucking your chin on to your chest will prevent your head from whiplashing into the ground. Rolling down is the softest way to meet the ground (as with parachuting) and keeping your arms and hands out of the way will prevent them from getting crushed and injured beneath your body.

To get to your feet as quickly as possible, incorporate the following move into the fall. As your back rolls on the ground and your legs swing up, tuck your head to one side and follow the impetus of the fall, letting your legs swing right over your head to bring you over into a kneeling position. Then get up quickly and face your assailant. The fall and the roll over up on to the feet should be one continuous movement.

When falling forwards, use the *judo forward roll*. Reach forward and down with your right arm, tuck your chin over towards your left

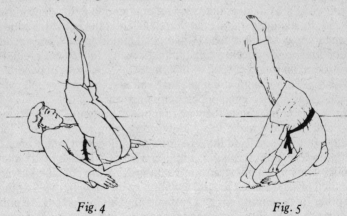

Fig. 4   Fig. 5

shoulder and dive forward rolling head-over-heels from your right shoulder to left hip. If you do a forward gymnastic roll, you will roll down the length of your spine; the judo one, however, rolls you diagonally from shoulder to hip. Continue the impetus of the roll and come back on to your feet, instantly turning around to face your assailant. During the roll your head should barely touch the ground (Fig. 5).

If you are pushed violently face down from behind you may not be able to roll forward. In this case the *forward break-fall* may absorb some of the shock of falling. When you are shoved violently to the ground there is the danger of hitting your face or your knees. To avoid this, angle the body as you go down so that your backside is the highest point from the ground and land on your two forearms (Fig. 6). On hard ground falling will be painful whatever you do, but the aim is always to minimise the shock of the fall. One benefit of using the forward break-fall is that you are reasonably placed to spring up and into action. Lying face down on the ground is probably the most vulnerable position you can be in. Practise this fall first of all from a kneeling position, then stand up spreading the legs very wide, then do it from a normal standing position.

One other way to fall when pushed from behind is to spin round so that you land on your back, taking care, as before, to keep your chin tucked in and your arms out of the way.

It may happen that you will stumble to the ground and not be able to make the break-fall and roll up on to your feet. In this case you must be especially careful how you get to your feet if the assailant is near. Having hit the floor, first swivel so that your feet are nearest to the

Fig. 6

assailant – head away from him. If necessary you can use them to kick out at him. Roll on to your right side, cross and bend your legs, left over right, prop yourself up with your right arm and hold your left hand out roughly in front of your face (Fig. 7). When the opportunity is right, spring from this position backwards into a kneeling crouch then rise quickly to your feet. The whole move must be done very carefully and quickly, taking care to protect your head with your left arm. (See also page 102 on bringing down a standing assailant from this position).

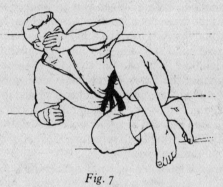

Fig. 7

Evasive movement

The shortest and therefore the fastest distance between two points is a straight line. Punches and kicks nearly always take this line. Anything moving powerfully in a straight line cannot easily change direction, so many of the self-defence moves in this book combine or start with a movement which takes the defender out of the line of the attack. The importance of this sort of move can be appreciated when dealing with a knife thrust to your body. If you stay where you are and attempt to deal with it but miss, the knife will go into you. If on the other hand you have moved out of the way, your failed counter-move will not necessarily result in your being stabbed. Moving out of line of the attack is a simple but very important move which must be practised countless times so that it becomes virtually automatic.

Mark off a line on the ground about seven or eight feet long. Get a training partner to face you a few feet away on the line. Stand on the line yourself. Slowly at first, get your partner to move along the line towards you holding his right hand out in front, as if thrusting with a knife. As his hand is just about to touch you, swing your right foot and side back and round in a quarter circle, pivoting on your left foot. Imagine that you are a door hinged down the left side and that your right side is swinging back and round. As you do this your partner should brush past you on his way along the line (Fig. 8). This is the basic move. Gradually you can speed it up and shorten the distance between you and your partner. Practise it also against a left-handed attack by pivoting to the other side of the line. Having made this evasive type of action, check that you have moved completely to one side of the marked off line.

A slightly more risky evasive action is to leave your feet on the line, but swivel your head and body off it. This is a faster move but you leave yourself less room to move.

Take care to practise on a line. Insufficient evasive action will then be obvious.

Another useful evasive movement is the *boxing side-step*. This is particularly useful if someone comes rushing at you swinging his

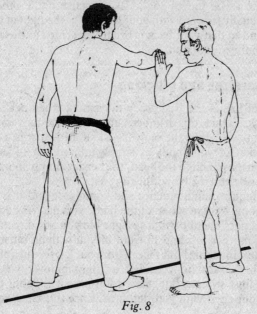

Fig. 8

arms. You can then move out of his path and straight-punch him as he moves past. Take up the Ready Stance – left foot forward, arms up. Stand across a line and face directly along it. As the assailant moves towards you, pull your forward left foot across the line and directly towards your right foot. It will be easier to do this if you have the heel of your right foot off the ground. Next, shoot your right foot directly sideways. Finally, turn slightly towards your left so as to face the assailant who should be moving straight along the line, and pull your left foot back slightly to assume a shoulder-width stance. This side-step takes some practice. From the assailant's point of view it is a very deceptive move.

Another type of evasive movement is the *spin turn* much used in karate or Kung Fu. Not only does the spin serve to confuse the assailant as to your intentions, but the spinning action can be used to generate a lot of force for such counter-actions as a kick or a punch.

Working on the line again, imagine an assailant moving along the line towards you. When he is about three feet away, step diagonally forward with your *right* foot to the left of the line and, using this as a pivot, spin right round to your left to bring you round facing the assailant's side as he moves past. Also practise it the other way, stepping diagonally forward with your left foot to the right of the line. Spinning round so that your back is briefly presented to the assailant can be very confusing for him.

Slipping, parrying and blocking

Moving out of line is the basic *body* movement when dealing with straight attacks. Once this has been mastered the movement can be refined to the point where the blow is just slipped, that is to say the attacked portion of your body is simply moved out of line. For example, against a punch to the head, the head is simply moved a few inches to one side and the blow whistles past.

This does require some practice and confidence and it is usually better to combine evasive action of the body with parrying actions of the arms. It is possible to parry a straight blow in any direction. Get your training partner to stand in front of you with an outstretched right arm almost touching your face. With your left forearm and hand you can push the arm to your left or right or over your head. Generally, against straight right-handed attacks it is better to parry the blow to your right with your left arm, since this takes you away from the attacker's left hand, and leaves your right hand free for counter-punching (see Fig. 22, page 37).

Against blows that curve towards your body, it is generally better to block them – that is to say, stop them dead in their tracks. As with parries this is best done with your forearm and hand (see Fig. 31, page 43).

It is very good self-defence training to practise slipping, parrying and blocking. Get your partner to make slow blows, as directed, and deal with them as above. Gradually, the practice can be speeded up. As in fencing, you only need to move and parry sufficiently out of the line of the attack. If you jump too wide you may be too far away to make your counter-move. Just let the hand or foot skim past you.

Basic counter-technique

After evasive action, most of the self-defence moves in this book finish with a throw, blow, lock or strangle hold. To avoid needless repetition, the general principles of such moves will be described below. They are essential moves and must be practised many times (see Chapter 11, on Self-defence Training).

Punching
1 The power of a punch comes from the hips and shoulders, not the arm. The arm only transmits the power. Learn to punch using the hips and shoulders.
2 Before actually striking, keep the arm and fist relaxed. A tense arm cannot move fast. On impact, clench the fist tightly and rotate (cork-screw) it round so that the palm faces down (straight punches).

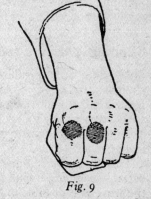

Fig. 9

3 Punch through the target.
4 Hit with the first two big knuckles of the hand (Fig. 9). Keep the thumb tucked out of the way, touching the forefinger between the first and second joints. On impact your knuckles, wrist and elbow should form a straight line.

Fig. 10

Fig. 11

5 Punch when advancing or stationary, not when moving backwards.
6 A straight punch (Fig. 10) is faster than a hooked one (Fig. 11); but a hooked one is very powerful and swings in from outside the line of vision.
7 Double up your punches, either head and body or right and left. Do not expect that one punch will do the trick. Put in a barrage.

Kicking

1 Raise the knee, as if stepping up on to a high box, flick the foot out (side, back or front) and pull it quickly back – the movement in one continuous whole (Figs 12 and 13).

Fig. 12

2 Stand straight, do not pull the hips back.
3 If wearing shoes, as you will be in most self-defence situations, kick with the toe-cap, but make your foot and ankle firm. Aim to connect with a particular part of your shoe or foot if you kick in any other manner.
4 For kicks higher than the groin, you will need to loosen up your ham-strings and hips. The lower you kick the quicker it will be.

Fig. 13

Throwing

1 A throw works best on a person who is off balance. Throw when he is rocking backwards on his heels or pitching forward on the balls of his feet. Make a sharp pull or push to get him there.
2 Use the assailant's movement. If he is rushing forward put something in front of him (i.e. your body) and pitch him over it and forwards (Fig. 14). If pulling back, put something behind him (i.e. your leg) and push him backwards (Fig. 15).
3 Focus the force of the throw by pushing down hard with your arms.
4 Take care not to fall over when throwing.
5 Lift the assailant up slightly before dropping him down. Bend and straighten the legs to achieve the lift.

Strangling

1 Aim to cut off the blood supply to the head, not the air to the lungs.
2 Move your hands or arms swiftly and strongly into the exact position. Once there you only have to hang on for a few seconds.
3 If rolling on the ground, trap the assailant between your legs as you apply the strangle.

Fig. 14

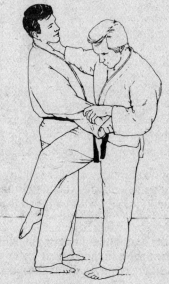

Fig. 15

Caution: Strangles can kill. If used to render someone unconscious, apply a strangle for no more than 12 seconds then release immediately. He will then take about 15–20 seconds to regain consciousness. Do not use against youngsters and those with high blood pressure or heart problems. Also check that the unconscious person does not choke on his own tongue or vomit. Use strangles only in extreme emergencies, such as when your life is threatened, and when level-headed. In the heat of the moment it is all too easy to misjudge the timing.

Joint-locking

1 Manipulate the limb and joint *quickly* and strongly into position. If the assailant has the chance to stiffen the attacked limb you will find it difficult to lock (see Figs 16–19).

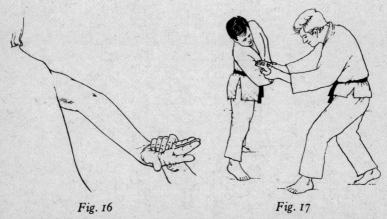

Fig. 16   *Fig. 17*

2 A light, quick blow to the face or other sensitive spot will often distract the assailant sufficiently for you to twist the limb.
3 Catch hold firmly and strongly with your hands using each finger fully.

An important point, not often understood with strangles and joint-locks, is that when the pain and threat to the throat or joint is immediate and intense there is only *one* thought and action, and that is to relieve the pain or threat. For example, with a strangle, if it takes immediate effect the victim will instantly try to rip the hands from his throat. Such will be the urgency of the situation that almost no other action is possible. Real threats limit all other actions. On the other hand, if the strangle or lock does not take immediate effect, the victim's hands or feet can be used to kick or punch.

Fig. 18

Fig. 19

The target

Some parts of the body are more sensitive than others. Being more sensitive they are often more difficult to hit since the protective reaction to a blow is also more sensitive and quick. Generally these parts of the body are well known. There are lesser known 'nerve spots' which if struck induce intense pain or temporary paralysis. These are often small spots and are difficult to strike accurately. A good example of a 'nerve spot' is the so-called 'funny-bone' in the elbow. As many people have experienced, if you accidentally hit your elbow in a certain way you can get a tingling shock in your forearm and hand. If you try to discover the exact spot you will have some difficulty. Many of the other nerve spots are equally difficult to find and, of course, to hit.

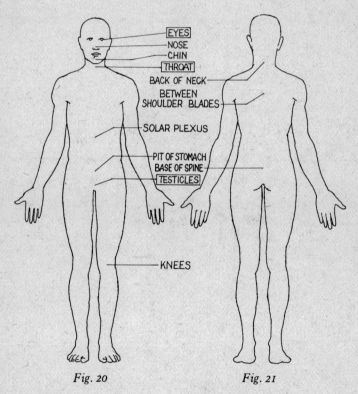

Fig. 20   Fig. 21

The three main sensitive targets on the front of the male assailant's body are the *eyes*, *throat* and *testicles*. Less sensitive, but equally vulnerable, are the chin, solar plexus, and the pit of the stomach. On the back of the body there are the back of the neck, between the shoulder blades, and the base of the spine. Other targets are the knees and the nose. Knees are especially vulnerable to kicks, and a blow to the nose, though not totally disabling, may deter many people from further violence.

When practising your self-defence blows, always try to aim at one of these targets. According to the seriousness of the situation, aim for the eyes, throat or testicles. Although you do not need a lot of strength to strike these spots, you must be fast and accurate, which demands a fair amount of practice. See the chart of vital spots (Figs 20 and 21).

4

Defences Against Punches and Kicks

Although there are many ways of kicking and punching in karate and boxing, the types of blow you may have to deal with in an everyday self-defence situation are few in number. They are: straight punch or hook to the head; straight punch or hook to the body; and a kick to the testicles or stomach. Theoretically, this number doubles since the attack may be with either the right or left fist. However, since most people are right-handed, practising against right-handed attacks will be mostly sufficient. For safety's sake, though, a certain amount of practice on the left is recommended (see Chapter 11).

Straight punch to the head

Defence One
A punch to the face is one of the most common assaults. The quickest reply to it is the boxing one – parry with the left and counter with the right.

As the assailant approaches to within striking distance, move into the Natural Stance and then into the Ready Stance, left side forward. As his right fist moves towards your face, intercept with your left hand and push the moving fist and wrist to your right so that it misses your face (Fig. 22). Combine this parry with a general evasive action of the body by stepping back and round with your right foot in a quarter-circle. Having parried the blow and stepped round, counter with a strong right-hand punch to the assailant's body or head (Fig. 23). Exactly where you counter depends on how the assailant is exposed. If

Fig. 22

Fig. 23

you have parried his attacking arm down, you may be able to punch his exposed face. If his arm is parried up, you may be able to hit his stomach. In either case a *hooked counter-punch* with the right hand will be effective. When making a hooked punch, the fist is not pushed straight at the assailant, but swings in from the side or underneath in a curve and the arm is held curved.

Do not parry and counter-punch at the same time. This is something that beginners tend to do. Parry and then counter-punch with a quick one-two movement.

Defence Two
This defence involves an off-balancing movement which then renders the assailant vulnerable to many types of counter-strikes and more than one blow. As the assailant punches towards your face, parry his arm upwards with the outside edge of your left wrist (Fig. 24). As you make the deflection, sink down a few inches so as to duck your head out of the line of the blow. The instant the parry is made, catch hold of the assailant's right sleeve and pull sideways and down, so as to bring the assailant off balance to his right (Fig. 25). Holding the assailant off

Fig. 24

Fig. 25

Fig. 26

balance on his right foot (Fig. 26), counter-punch with your right fist either to his body or head. Follow up if necessary with another punch.

If you get the timing right the assailant may stumble to the floor from the impetus of his missed punch. However, it is probably easier to make a counter-blow when he is off balance in a standing position rather than when he is on the floor. Those who wish merely to learn how to avoid the blow could practise the deflection and pull, with the sole aim of stumbling the assailant to the floor. Otherwise keep him on his feet.

Defence Three

This defence is against an opponent who throws a right punch to your head. The evasive action in this case is to move your head so that the blow slips over your left shoulder. This type of evasive action is best done from fairly close in. As the violence threatens, adopt the Ready Stance.

As the assailant drives forward with his right fist towards your face, move your head a few inches to your right so that the fist and arm slip over your left shoulder. Combine this slip with a step in closer to the assailant with your left foot (Fig. 27). As you step in close, catch hold

Fig. 27

of the assailant with both arms. Take your left arm around his waist and catch hold of his left arm with your right hand. Push your hips across in front of his and swing him up on to your left hip (Fig. 28). Continue the action by swinging him over and down to the ground. Make sure that he is lifted up and over your hips, not merely dragged round the side of your left leg. The lifting action in the final throw is like that in Fig. 14 (page 31).

Fig. 28

Push at face

In this attack the assailant is not out to injure your face with a punch, but is contemptuously shoving the palm of his hand in your face to push you away. The palm of the hand (Fig. 29), especially the heel of the hand, can be quite an effective weapon when pushed into the face. It can be pushed violently into the face or up under the nose, or brought close quite slowly then accelerated in from a short distance. Try placing the tips of your fingers on a desk top, then abruptly crash down the heel of the hand. You will see that quite a lot of force can be generated. Knowing this, be especially careful of open hands moving towards your face.

Various defences can be applied against this sort of attack. The following defence takes advantage of the fact that the assailant is trying to push you away, rather than punching, and so will be putting his weight behind the push. As the right hand nears your face, push it up in the air with the outside of your left wrist. The impetus of the assailant's push will carry him slightly forward, giving you the opportunity to duck under his arm. As you go under the arm and

Fig. 29

emerge slightly behind the assailant, follow up with a sharp strike with your right elbow to his kidneys (Fig. 30). Having made the elbow strike, turn around to face him, or move slightly further forward before turning.

Fig. 30

Hook to the head

A boxer's hook to the head can be a short, sharp, nasty blow. On the other hand the crude 'haymaker' type of blow, often seen in brawls, is fairly easy to deal with. This circular blow is easily blocked, which gives opportunities to catch hold of the arm as well as to counter-punch.

Adopt the Ready Stance. As the assailant's right arm swings round to your head, raise your left forearm to about face height and intercept the blow (Fig. 31). Instantly catch hold of the arm with your left hand, jump quickly round, also catching hold with your right arm, and flip the assailant over your back and right shoulder to the ground (Fig. 32). When you jump round, take care to turn so that your back touches the assailant's stomach. If the throwing movement to the ground is at all blocked in the standing position, quickly drop your *right* knee to the floor and pull him over your shoulder as before (Fig. 62).

An alternative to the throw is a right-hand punch to the assailant's stomach after you have blocked the blow.

Fig. 31

Fig. 32

Uppercut

The uppercut, either to the chin or the body, is a very powerful punch. In boxing it is the stock-in-trade of the tall boxer when faced with a shorter opponent. It is usually done from fairly close or very close in. The uppercut is a hooked punch that 'cuts' up from underneath either to the body or to the jaw in a circular swing.

One simple defence to this type of blow is simply to move back slightly so that the blow whistles past. This is a slightly negative move since it minimises your opportunity to counter-attack.

One good defence is to use the *forearm-block*. Adopt the Ready Stance. As the assailant starts to swing in with the blow, drop your left forearm strongly down into the crook of the assailant's right elbow. This will stop the punch dead and you will be in a position to counter-punch with your right hand, either to the head or body depending on which is exposed.

Straight punch to stomach

The defence against this attack is virtually the same as the first defence against a straight punch to the head. That is to say, parry with the left and counter with your right hand.

Adopt the Ready Stance. As the assailant's fist moves towards your stomach, step back and round in a quarter-circle with your right foot and side, and with your left hand push his fist and wrist to your right so that it slides past your stomach. As you parry the punch follow up with a counter-punch, straight right, or hook to his face.

Control moves, i.e. joint-locks, against a straight punch are rather difficult. Get a training partner to throw a few quick straight punches at you and try to catch the wrist or the arm. You will discover how difficult it is. On the other hand, learning to parry straight punches and kicks is fairly simple. Take care to parry first and then counter-punch. Do not do both at the same time.

Hook to the body

In this attack the assailant makes a curved punch or hook round to the side of your body or further round to the kidneys. The kidney punch is banned in boxing since a strong blow can rupture the kidneys, which can be fatal. With a little practice, hooks to the body can easily be stopped. The way to block the hook to the body is with the effective use of your elbows. Adopt the Ready Stance, with your hands extended. In this position there is room under both of your arms to hook in with either a left or a right. However, this can easily be blocked by simply pulling the elbows back in to the body. By moving either of the elbows lower, near to or away from the centre of the body, you can block off all blows to that region. From the elbow-block, either counter with a right hook to the body or face, or throw the assailant to the ground by hooking your right leg round the back of his and pushing him backwards (Fig. 15) with your right hand on his throat.

It is also possible to use the elbows to block the kidney punch. In this case do not move the elbows into the body but back along the side of the body in combination with a slight twist of the hips so as to take the attacked side of the body back away from the punch. Alternatively, from the Ready Stance, push your left *hand* down and out to the side. This will intercept the hook (Fig. 33). Follow this up by then

Fig. 33

Fig. 34

stepping in closer to the assailant with your left foot and catching him round the waist with your left arm. At the same time catch hold of his left arm or sleeve. Spin round on the spot and place the back of your hips across the front of his and lift him up in the air by straightening your legs (Fig. 34). Continue the action by swinging him over your hips and dropping him heavily to the ground.

When blocking the kidney punch in this way, take care to intercept the blow wide of your body. It is not difficult to misjudge the distance since the blow is curling in all the time.

Kick to the stomach

Defence One

One of the simplest defences against any kick is to jump back out of reach. If a person attacks with his fists he can move in fast as he punches, but, when kicking, the attacker is rooted to the spot since he needs one leg to stand on as the other is doing the kicking. Thus it is a fairly simple matter just to jump back out of reach as you see the foot coming up.

Fig. 35

To counter a kick to the stomach, use the moving-off-the-line evasive movement. From the Natural or Ready Stance, pivot on your left foot, swinging your right side and foot back round in a quarter-circle. As you swing back, hook your left arm and swing it under the heel and lower calf of the kicking leg, lifting it slightly so as to trap it (Fig. 35). Having caught the leg, the simplest move is to push the assailant's leg violently up in the air with both your arms so that he is flung backwards to the ground.

When catching the leg, do not try to catch it with your hand, it will not be strong enough. Hook underneath the kicking leg with hand, wrist and forearm and cradle it with that general area.

Defence Two

Instead of hurling the assailant to the ground as in the previous defence, this one attempts to control him with a leg-lock. As the foot swings up, pivot on your left foot and move out of line, swinging your

Fig. 36

right foot and side back in a quarter-circle. At the same time, hook your left arm as before and slide it under the kicking leg so as to catch it low on the calf. Keeping the leg propped up in the air, swing your body slightly back the way it came, at the same time encircling the leg with your right arm going round the lower leg and ankle area. Join the hands together, with the assailant's right foot trapped under your right armpit. At this point he will probably fall to the ground. If he does not, simply push him over, but in either case take care to maintain a tight hold on the leg (Fig. 36).

Having caught the leg, apply pressure to it by pushing the bony part of your thumb side of the wrist and lower right forearm into his Achilles tendon and leaning backwards so as to lever the leg upwards. Either control him in this position or try for a *one-legged Boston-crab* (see page 101).

Defence Three
Sometimes you will not have time or space to move out of the line of the attack. You will have to react directly to the kick. One of the

Fig. 37

easiest blocks to a kick is the *cross-arm block*.

As the assailant lashes out with his foot, punch down with both fists so that they cross over and form a V-shape (Fig. 37). Aim your punch so that the V-shape intercepts the lower shin of the kicking leg. The wider you make the V-shape, the more chance you will have to intercept the kick. However, do not make the block too wide, as the foot may connect with your stomach. To make sure that this does not happen, pull your stomach and hips back a little as you make the block.

To follow up this block try to catch the leg. If you have punched down with your right arm over the top of your left, pivot on your *right* foot, pulling your left side and foot back so that you almost turn your back to the assailant. As you turn round catch hold of the leg with your right arm and lift it up. If the leg is held high enough he will be off balance and unable to punch at you. From this semi-back-on position, balance on your left leg and with your right leg hook the back of your knee round the back of his left knee and hook his leg off the ground towards you. This will send him crashing heavily to the ground.

This cross-arm block can be used to stop a kick to the testicles. Since the target is lower, you will have to punch lower and spread your legs so as to drop slightly. Otherwise the movement is virtually the same as the one above.

One other simple block to a kick to the testicles is to lift the knee high and swing the leg across in front of the other one. This means taking some of the discomfort of the kick on your own leg but this is preferable to having your testicles kicked. From this raised leg position it is then possible to make a snap side-kick back at the assailant.

Defence Four
With a little practice kicks can be easily parried, as distinct from being blocked. Which side you deflect the kick to depends on your initial stance. If in the Ready Stance with your left leg forward, use your left hand to deflect the kick out to your left. When you make the deflection try briefly touching your right shoulder with the tips of your left fingers, then lash your arm down to the side, making contact with the assailant's leg either with an open hand or a clenched fist (Fig. 38). In either case make contact with the little finger edge of your left hand. Exactly the same parry can be made when you are standing square-on

Fig. 38

Fig. 39

to your assailant. In this case step back with your right foot as he starts to kick and deflect the leg as above with your left arm.

When deflecting the kick to the right of your body there is more of a problem. Usually an assailant will kick with his right leg and your left hand will be nearer to it to make the parry. If you are going to parry the kick with your right hand, the assailant's leg will have to be more over to the right side of your body. Alternatively, he may kick with his left leg. Judgment as to which way you deflect the kick depends on the position of the assailant's leg. If it is to the right side of your body, deflect to the right (Fig. 39), and *vice versa*. Whichever side you deflect to, the action is the same – a solid sweep down with your arm to intercept the leg.

Some discomfort may be felt in your hand and forearm as you make the parry, since a leg is quite a heavy object. Nevertheless, if you deflect rather than block the kick it will not be that uncomfortable.

5

Defences Against Grapple Attacks

Often in the self-defence situation an assailant will catch hold of you, either to force you to do something, or to steady you prior to making a blow. There are a number of ways in which he can do this and it is necessary to know what to do in each case. The ways you can be caught

Fig. 40

hold of can be divided roughly into three groups: wristgrabs, front holds and rear holds. Wristgrabs are often used when an assailant wants to twist the victim's arms or drag him somewhere. How you are held often depends on what clothes you are wearing. If there is a lot of cloth available the assailant can grab virtually anywhere. If the assailant holds fairly low the grip can often be easily broken by using one of your knees to smash down on his wrist (Fig. 40).

One point to appreciate with grapple attacks is that, unless you are used to manhandling bodies as a wrestler or judo fighter, you can easily be knocked off balance or be surprised by the weight and strength of the assailant. If you practise the grapple defences enough you will learn to keep your balance and get used to heavy bodies. Alternatively, practise some judo.

Wristgrab (crossgrip)

The assailant grabs your right wrist with a crossgrip (as with a handshake) (Fig. 41). Immediately straighten the fingers, making

Fig. 41

your arm strong from fingertips to elbow. Keeping your lower arm firm, twist your hand and fingers round in a clockwise direction to catch hold of the assailant's wrist. Hold it tightly and push strongly with your left hand against the back of his elbow (Fig. 42), straightening his arm and forcing him flat to the floor (Fig. 18). To maintain control of the assailant, kneel on his triceps with your right knee, just above the point of the elbow. If, after you have grabbed his wrist, his arm bends into an L-shape, simply push the point of the elbow round and down to the floor and control him as before. If the whole move is done violently enough, the assailant may be crashed to the floor knocking any further fight out of him.

Fig. 42

Wristgrab (same side)

This time the assailant grabs your right wrist with his left hand. Point the fingers, making the arm strong from the elbow to the fingertips, pull your elbow into your side and extend your forearm strongly out from the body, palm uppermost (as if carrying a tray). Pivoting on your right foot, swing your left foot and side back and round, so as to bring your right shoulder into contact with the assailant's left shoulder. As you pivot round, keep your hand in the tray-carrying position and your movement will automatically wrest your wrist from his grasp (Fig. 43). If you make your lower arm firm as described, the turning action of your *body* breaks the grip.

Once you have broken the grip you can follow up by making your hand into a fist and flicking the back of it into the assailant's face. This is done from where you stand close to the assailant. Alternatively, step away slightly then kick back sideways into the side of his knee.

Fig. 43

Double wristgrab

Defence One

In this attack both of the assailant's hands grab one of your wrists. As with all wristgrabs, the tendency for the untrained person is simply to pull back away from the hold. However, the attacker's grasp is strong in this direction. The weak point in most holds is the thumb and the way to break a hold is to exert leverage against the thumb. The double wristgrab is easily broken in this way.

Reach over the top of your trapped wrist and clasp your hands together. To break the hold lift your clasped hands up towards your face and push your lower elbow in towards the assailant's stomach (Fig. 44) as if making a blow with it. The hold will then easily shatter. The important part of the defence is to move your elbow in towards

Fig. 44

the stomach. Do not just pull your clasped hands directly away from the grip. Having broken the hold, follow up, if necessary, with a punch, kick or throw.

Defence Two

In the previous situation one of your wrists was seized by both the assailant's hands, but held in the way a rope would be held if climbing it. In this situation, one of your wrists is seized by both the assailant's hands but in a different way. Imagine a horizontal bar in front of you which you catch hold of, both sets of fingers curling over the top of the bar and both thumbs underneath. Approaching from the right side, the assailant has caught hold of your right wrist and forearm in the above manner.

Although you are caught by both the assailant's hands, the release from this hold is similar to that of the crossgrip on the single wrist. Point your right fingers down to the floor, making your whole lower arm strong, then twist your hand and fingers round in a clockwise semi-circle in exactly the same way as shown in Fig. 42 (page 55), so as to catch his right wrist. Having caught the wrist, push his right arm in towards his body so that it forms an L-shape, then push his elbow, which will be sticking up, round and down towards the ground (Fig. 19). This will cause pain to his arm and shoulder joint and force him to the floor. Either make this move so abruptly that he is crashed to the floor, or do it smoothly so that he is brought under control to the floor.

Defence Three

This time the assailant grabs both of your wrists, one in each hand. It is possible to kick at him, although, if you are being pulled, there is a good chance that you will be off balance, making a kick difficult. To release the hold, proceed as follows.

With as much impetus as possible, shoot your right hand across and grab hold of the assailant's right wrist, breaking his grip and freeing your left hand (Fig. 45). Next pull his right hand across your body

Fig. 45

Fig. 46

from left to right. This will almost turn him away from you (Fig. 46). Complete the turn by using your left arm on his left shoulder to pull it towards you. As you pull the arm across your body, also step round behind the assailant as he turns. Once behind him, follow up by either wrapping your left arm round his throat and trying for a strangle (see the Sleeper, page 140), or kick the back of his right knee forwards and pull him to the ground.

Defence Four

In this situation the assailant has caught hold of your wrists, as with the previous defence, but has not started to pull. Seize the initiative and step back suddenly with your right foot, and at the same time swing both of your arms up and out to your sides. This combination of moves should bring him off balance forward, with his upper body and head dipped down. Before he has time to let go and recover his balance and position, either knee him abruptly in the face with your right knee (Fig. 47) or kick him in the stomach. Which you do depends on how much his head will have been brought down. This sort of move must be done a split second after the assailant has taken hold, and before he has time to stiffen up.

Fig. 47

Defence Five

This time your wrists are caught from underneath and are held up fairly high in the air (Fig. 48). The release move is similar to the previous one but is more effective, due to the different position of the assailant's hands. As soon as your wrists are caught, swing your fists towards each other, then down and round and out in one big circle. As your hands swing out to the side of your body, the assailant will be forced to release his grip (Fig. 49). At this point there are a number of counter-move options, such as punching and kicking. However, in this case, drive the crown of your head into the assailant's solar plexus and at the same time snatch his legs forward, gripping behind both knees (Fig. 50). Not only will the butt to his solar plexus be effective (see Stomach Butt, page 134) but the combined action should drop him very heavily to the floor.

As in all these two-stage moves there should be no appreciable gap between each move. The timing must be a quick one-two.

Fig. 48

Fig. 49

Fig. 50

Single lapel grab

Defence One

Quite often an assailant will grab your lapel with his left hand and
threaten to hit you with his right. The instant he takes hold, reach up
with your right hand and catch hold of his hand (not the wrist) with
your fingers curling over the fleshy part of the thumb and with your
own thumb at the back of his hand. Simultaneously, push the palm of
your left hand into the assailant's face (Fig. 51). This does not have to
be done particularly violently, just enough to distract him. Having
gripped his hand, twist it in a clockwise direction, bringing in your left
hand to reinforce the action (see Fig. 17, page 32). This will instantly
cause pain to the wrist and force him off balance. Continue the
twisting action, forcing him to the ground. As with all joint-locks, you
can either break the hold and escape, maintain control, or incapacitate
the joint by cracking the wrist-twist on sharply.

With all the wrist-twists it is important to understand the exact grip
on the hand. The lower arm can be likened to a spoon-shaped object.
If such an object were embedded in concrete and you wanted to loosen
it, you would grasp the spoon end and twist backwards and forwards.
This would give you the best leverage. You would not grasp the stem

Fig. 51

of the object. Similarly, when applying the wrist-twist you must grasp the hand and twist, not the wrist.

Defence Two

This move also can be applied to someone putting his hand on your chest to push you away. As with the previous move, the assailant reaches up and catches hold of one or both of your lapels. The hold does not have much purpose save perhaps to pull you forwards or threaten you with a punch. Nevertheless, once the assailant has caught hold of you, he acquires a certain amount of control and is psychologically one step ahead. He must be answered immediately.

A fairly uncomplicated move is as follows: the instant he catches hold, reach up with both your hands and cup them over the assailant's right hand and pin it to your chest. Press the little finger edges of your hands into the line where the hand meets the forearm. It does not matter too much which way the hand is pinned to your chest. A lot will depend on how flexible the assailant's wrist is. Either pin the hand, palm facing outwards, or the other way, palm facing or touching your chest.

Having pinned the hand, step back with your left foot and lean forward with your upper body so as to bear down on the wrist (Fig. 52). This will cause pain to the wrist and force him to the ground. To follow up the move, knee the assailant in the body with your right knee.

Fig. 52

Double lapel grab

An assailant may grab both of your lapels with both of his hands merely to threaten or shake you. Often, however, the double lapel grab is a prelude to a very vicious attack, namely a head butt to your nose and face. The head butt is a very quick move and difficult to avoid. Your defences against the hold must include something that would stop the head butt.

The *instant* your lapels are grabbed reach over the assailant's two arms with your right arm and catch hold of his right hand curling your fingers round the little finger edge. To do this you will have to reach round quite far but this will position your elbow so that it blocks the path of any butt (Fig. 53). As you grasp the hand, simultaneously make some distracting move such as a kick in the shins or groin. Having grasped the hand, twist it in a clockwise direction (Fig. 16) bringing up your left hand to reinforce the action. As you twist, the pain in the wrist will force him to let go and turn him around. If he turns round and his twisted wrist and arm fold into the small of his back, bring him to the ground by kicking the back of his right knee forward with your right foot. Then immobilise him as with the Immobilisation technique described on page 135.

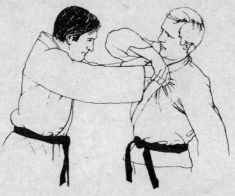

Fig. 53

Alternatively, continue to twist the wrist but pull the assailant's arm away from his body. With the wrist twisted and pulled away from the body, you will be able to control him in a standing position. Do not simply let the arm fold into the small of the back, as he may then escape from the wrist hold. With this and the previous wrist-twists, hold with a grip of steel. Feel each finger pressing into the assailant's hands.

Front strangle

A strangle is an apparently easy attack to counter. Your arms and legs are free for kicking and punching, and the assailant's body is unprotected. However, if hands are biting into your neck your one thought will be to release that pressure and you will probably instinctively bring your hands up to your neck to break the grip. This may waste valuable seconds, especially if the attacker's hands are strong. You do not have long.

Defence One

Your first move must be to relieve the pressure on your neck. First tighten your neck muscles and sink your head into your shoulders, bring the shoulders up to the ears and the chin down towards the collar-bone. This will ease some of the pressure.

To break the grip on your throat, swing your right arm violently over the assailant's two arms and pivot strongly about a quarter-turn to your left (Fig. 54). Made abruptly this move will shatter the grip round your neck. Do not just swing the arm over but combine it with a powerful twist of your body. As a follow-up, swing your right elbow back and jab it in the assailant's face.

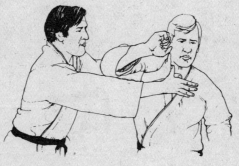

Fig. 54

If you are being strangled but have been pushed up against a wall you will not be able to move as above. Instead, hunch the neck as before and push your forefinger and middle finger into the hollow beneath the assailant's Adam's Apple and just above the collar-bones. Push strongly and this will force him to release the hold. As he does so, move away from the wall and follow up with a kick or a punch if necessary.

Defence Two

When a strangler starts to apply pressure to your neck his arms will almost certainly widen as he uses more strength. This will bring him closer to you and leave his face and neck exposed. It may not be possible to press into the hollow below the Adam's Apple, as in the previous defence, for example if there is a coat or heavy clothing in the

Fig. 55

way. However, some of the neck will almost certainly be exposed. In this case, to break the stranglehold jab into his neck with your fingertips (Fig. 55). It is a soft target and there is no likelihood of your hurting the fingers. When making the jab, extend the fingers strongly and keep them close up against each other for extra strength. Also tuck the thumb in. If by any chance you miss the target it is possible to injure the thumb should it catch on clothing.

Defence Three

With this defence against a strangle you utilise the assailant's strong arms to throw him to the ground. It is a peculiar fact that if someone catches hold of an object and you try to wrest it from his grasp he will hold on tighter, even though holding on endangers him. There is a reluctance to let go which occasionally can be used in self defence. Conversely, it is the mark of a person skilled in self defence that he can let a bad situation go instantly.

As the assailant grabs your neck, tense it and rock back and forwards slightly so as to make him hang on tighter. Quickly reach up with both arms, taking your left one over the assailant's right arm, and your right arm under his left and clasp your hands together. At this point you should be standing with your feet about shoulder-width apart, square on to the assailant. Pivoting on your left foot, turn to your left and swing your right foot across in front of your left, placing the lower part of your right calf against the assailant's right lower shin. As you turn around, lever up the assailant's left arm with your right

Fig. 56

and push down on his right with your left (Fig. 56). Continue the action with your arms as you turn around and this will send the assailant spinning to the floor.

If by any chance the assailant should let go his grip when you are half-way through the move, be prepared to follow up with a right elbow jab.

Side strangle

It may happen that an assailant approaches from the side and tries to strangle you. If the assailant's hands are large and your neck is small it does not make a lot of difference to him which angle he strangles from, but it does alter your defence move.

As the assailant's hands tighten round your neck lift your arm on the side nearest to him and take it up *between* the two arms. Raise it high then swing it *back* down and round so as to encircle one of the assailant's arms.

As you encircle it his elbow will bend inwards causing considerable pain in the joint. Join your hands together and keep the pressure on the elbow. By now the stranglehold will have been shattered and you must decide whether to wreck the joint or keep the assailant under control.

When you encircle the arm take care that your encircling arm pressures the assailant's elbow and does not slide up under his armpit or down to his wrist.

Front embrace

Defence One
This assault may take two forms. Either the assailant wraps both arms over and round your two arms and upper body, or, in the case of women victims, one arm round the neck, the other round the waist.

In either case, counter the hold by bringing the knee swiftly up into the attacker's testicles (Fig. 57). This may not disable him but it will certainly force him to let go. If needs be, follow up with a kick or punch.

Alternative moves in this situation are to stamp on the top of the assailant's foot or bite him.

Fig. 57

Defence Two

Another way to break the hold when the attacker wraps both arms round your upper arms and shoulders from the front is to put pressure on the sensitive area just under the nose.

As the attacker takes hold, reach round his waist with your right arm and take a tight hold. Reach up with your left arm over his right arm and place the palm of your hand directly under his nose. To break the hold, push strongly into the area where the underside of the nose meets the upper lip, forcing the attacker's head away and down and at the same time pull his hips forward with your other arm. This will cause pain under the nose and discomfort in the back, forcing him to release the hold. If you continue to push, the attacker will eventually lose balance and drop to the ground.

If you find it awkward to push the palm of your hand under the nose, try the little finger edge of the same hand. Whatever you do, take care that the attacker does not turn his head sideways to slide the hand off his face. To avoid this the move must be made swiftly and resolutely.

Bear hug

With this attack the victim is grabbed round the rib cage, under the arms, and is squeezed or lifted up. The attacker's intention may be to damage the ribs or back, or to carry the victim off.

Fig. 58

As the attacker catches hold you may find it possible to knee him in the testicles, but once lifted or squeezed backwards you may find this difficult. If lifted or squeezed, insert the thumbs or forefingers of each hand into the corners of the attacker's mouth and pull sideways (Fig. 58). This will cause him to let go instantly. Alternatively push your thumbs into the hollow just behind each earlobe.

If necessary, follow up swiftly with a punch, kick or throw.

Front neck-hold

Quite often an assailant will not catch hold of your wrists or lapels, but will throw one arm around the back of your neck to pull you forward or wrestle you to the ground. This is an indefinite sort of attack, but quite common. The fact that the assailant has reached right round your neck means that he will be quite close and therefore vulnerable to close-quarter defences. In this case the elbow can be used effectively. As soon as the arm goes round your neck, swing your right elbow up, and strike the assailant under the jaw (Fig. 59). Do not simply push

Fig. 59

the elbow up, but swing it round and up, pivoting from the shoulder. The movement is deceptive and can catch an assailant unawares.

It is essential when countering the neck-hold to keep your own head and neck straight. If your head gets pulled down you will be unable to make the counter-move.

If you do not wish to defend yourself with a blow, the proximity of your assailant will make it easy to pull off throws, such as on page 31.

Arm around shoulder

This situation applies when an assailant approaches from the side and puts one arm around your shoulders. It probably applies more to women victims than to men.

Your immediate weapon is your elbow. It is most likely that you will be approached from your left side if the assailant is right-handed, in which case you will have to use your left elbow.

Turn your hand palm upwards and either clench the fist or strongly extend the fingers. Next, accelerate the point of your elbow sideways into the lower ribs of the assailant below his armpit. Make sure that you strike with the point of your elbow and that you dig it in very sharply. Unless you have an extremely powerful elbow jab, it is unlikely that this will incapacitate the assailant. Follow the move up by swinging round to face the man and do the *Back heel* throw (Fig. 15, page 31) on him, or run away.

Elbow jabs are very efficient close-quarter weapons. They look easy, but do require some practice to acquire explosion and sharpness.

Another useful move in this position is to stamp hard on the top of the assailant's foot and follow up with the throw as above.

Arm grab from rear-side

An assailant approaches quietly from behind and grips your arm above the elbow. This is not a dangerous move in itself, but is preparatory to a threat or something more unpleasant.

Step slightly away from the assailant and make a low kick with the outside edge of your shoe into the side of the knee (Fig. 60). This is a nasty but effective move. As with the elbow jab, some practice is required to make it sharp, hard and accurate. Practise the kick against a tree or post positioned off to your side or rear.

A knee kick may not be appropriate, in which case try the following control move. After your arm has been gripped, swing your whole arm backwards and up under the assailant's armpit. Continue the circular action, bringing your hand up and round the rear of his shoulder and forward again so as to encircle the arm. Push forward against his now encircled arm and force him forwards off balance to the ground.

The above two defences are against someone who is standing more or less at your side, not someone standing directly behind you. If he is directly behind, an elbow jab will be appropriate, as will a knee kick, although this will be more difficult if you cannot see the knee.

Fig. 60

Rear strangle

Defence One

This can be an extremely difficult and dangerous move to counter, especially if you are off balance. As with the front strangle, ease the immediate pressure on the neck by tensing your neck, lifting the shoulders and pulling the chin down towards the collar-bone (Fig. 61).

Fig. 61

The immediate problem will be to recover your balance. This will depend a lot on how your attacker is standing. If he is behind you with his legs spread fairly wide, drive your right leg back through his legs and push into him with your backside. If you feel one of his legs pushing into yours, recover your balance by twisting to your right.

As you tense your neck and recover balance, reach up with both hands and grasp the strangling arm and pull down away from the pressure on the neck.

To finish off the defence, drop your right knee *suddenly* to the floor, hold tight to his arm, and either roll him directly over your shoulder (if you have been able to step back through his legs) or stumble him to the ground (if you have twisted to the side) (Fig. 62). In either case, drop to the floor as swiftly as you can. This should send him hurtling off balance and down. Tense your neck, recover balance and drop in one continuous move.

If the assailant is strangling from behind with his *hands* (not the whole arm round your neck), whiplash round to your right, swinging your right arm round in a big circle, and strike with the edge of your hand, karate-chop style, against the side of his head or into his ribs.

Fig. 62

Defence Two

When an assailant is strangling you from close behind, he is theoretically open to various close-quarter defences. There are two problems
with this type of attack. The first is that you may be pulled off balance,
and the second is that the assailant is more or less out of sight. In both
cases it may be difficult for you to hit him. However, depending upon
circumstances, you may not lose your balance, in which case there are
a number of ways to hit the assailant. Since you cannot see him you
will have to rely on feel to guide you to the target, and you will only
succeed if you practise the basic situation several times.

As the assailant stands behind you, your elbows, head and feet are
your main weapons. When making the elbow defence, clench your fist,
palm uppermost, and accelerate the point of your elbow into his ribs,
stomach or solar plexus. Which elbow you use depends on how the
assailant stands behind you. If he is slightly to your right side move
your hips and body to the left and hit with your right elbow, and *vice
versa*.

The use of the head also depends on the position of the attacker's
head in relation to your own. If it is directly behind, crack the back of
your head into his nose and face. You do not need much room to do
this, but it must be done sharply.

Similarly, your feet can be used to do a number of things. Look first
for opportunities to stamp on his toes or the bridge of his feet or,
secondly, try raking the side of your shoe down one of his shins.

If caught in a real-life situation, try first of all to use the elbows, then the head and finally the feet in fairly quick succession. You will have to explode into action very rapidly.

Defence Three
In this defence the assailant has not caught your neck too firmly, and you have managed to catch his arm with both your hands and pull it a little way from your throat.

Having caught the arm, continue to pull the arm down your chest and away from your throat. When you get it low enough, change your left-hand grip so that you grip his wrist from above, your fingers facing out and your thumb between the assailant's arm and your body. Lever the arm slightly away from your body and slide your right hand, in the same grip, down towards your left, tucking your right thumb round the wrist to meet your fingers.

Holding tightly on to the wrist with both hands, duck out backwards under the assailant's right armpit, twisting his arm in a clockwise direction as you do so. The twisting action on the arm will bring the assailant totally under control. If the twisting action brings the assailant's arm folded into the small of his back, kick him in the back of the right knee and drop him to the ground. (The action is similar to that of the Irish Whip, Fig. 115, page 145.)

Over-arm grab from rear

If someone jumps on you from behind, encircling your arms, you will probably lose balance. Recover your balance quickly by dropping your weight a few inches and spreading your legs wide front to back.

Breaking the arm hold is a simple matter. Reach back with either hand and grasp or poke the testicles of the assailant (Fig. 63). Alternatively, dig your fingers into his groin or inguinal fold. His instant reaction will be to let go. Once he lets go follow up with an elbow-jab to his solar plexus or stomach. Otherwise you can catch hold of his right arm with your two arms and throw him forward over your shoulder, as on page 73.

Another move which breaks the grip is to drop your weight and spread your legs wide as before, combined with a violent lift of both arms sideways to shoulder height (Fig. 64). If all three actions are done sharply and simultaneously the hold can be shattered. Then follow up with an elbow-jab.

Fig. 63

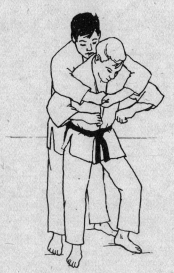

Fig. 64

Under-arm grab from rear

The reason for this type of attack may be that the attacker wishes to pick you up, either to dash you to the floor or carry you off somewhere. The attack can be countered in a number of ways.

Defence One
The easiest way to shatter the hold is to catch hold of the assailant's little fingers and bend them outwards (Fig. 65). As the assailant feels the threat to his fingers he will probably snatch them away. This will then leave him open to an elbow-jab to the head. If you do, however, manage to keep a hold of a little finger, continue to bend it. This will keep control of the assailant. It is not difficult to dislocate a little finger and it is amazing how incapacitating such a small dislocation can be.

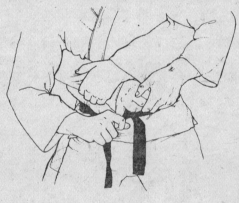

Fig. 65

If the assailant is obviously trying to carry you off and his little fingers are inaccessible, bend forwards from the waist and let your upper body flop down as if touching your toes. This will turn your body into an unmanageable object, virtually impossible to carry. When bent forward in this way, look through your legs and, if you see one of the assailant's legs close by, reach through both your legs and pull his leg forward. This will make him stumble backwards. As he goes backwards, take care to fall on him as heavily as possible, then rapidly disengage and stand up.

Fig. 66

Defence Two

This defence relies on being able to strike an extremely small nerve spot in the back of the hand. When an assailant wraps his arms around your middle he may clasp his two hands together so that the back of one of them faces outwards and slightly up. If he does so, make a fist and protrude the large middle finger so that the second knuckle from the finger tip sticks out about half an inch more than the rest, but otherwise keep the fist (Fig. 66). Use the sharp point of this knuckle to strike the nerve spot found in the back of the hand. The exact position of it can be found as follows. Make a fist and run your finger along the groove between the bones of the index finger and the middle finger in the back of the hand. Where the groove ends there is a slight indentation and this is the spot to strike. Light experimentation on your own hand will show how sensitive the spot is. When an assailant's hand is struck quite sharply his grip will break instantly, and if struck sharply enough will paralyse the hand.

Head in chancery

This was an old boxing move much used before the present Queensbury rules were formulated: its name refers to an ancient English law court from which it was regarded as extremely difficult to extricate oneself once legally embroiled. The assailant may catch your head under his arm and either punch you in the face or wrestle you to the ground. With your head caught in this way it can be extremely difficult to free yourself without recourse to vicious measures.

One effective measure is to grasp or punch the assailant's testicles with either hand. The left hand can go through the legs from behind or your right hand can punch directly at them.

Another method is to reach up with your left hand over the assailant's shoulder and sink your fingers, clawlike, into his face. Using this grip pull his head backwards and down, lifting his right leg up with your right arm (Fig. 67) to make him stumble roughly to the ground. As soon as you feel the slightest loosening of his hold around your neck, snatch your head free.

If by some mischance you should end up on the ground with your head still trapped, try to force the assailant's head as far away as possible from his shoulder and the arm which is holding your head. You may be able to do this by using the clawlike grip on his face or catching hold of his hair, or by swinging a leg over his head. The more you can force his head away, the weaker the grip round your neck will become, giving you the chance to free yourself.

You might get caught in the reverse of this hold, that is, with your head caught under the armpit facing his rear. This is an extremely dangerous hold since, if the assailant knows what he is doing, he can break your neck. Freeing yourself is not an easy business. If there is not too much pressure on your neck, try striking the assailant's testicles. Alternatively, drop your right knee to the ground, straight-

Fig. 67

ening your head as you do so, thrust your right arm through the assailant's legs and catch hold of his right thigh. Lifting your head and straightening your back, lift the assailant off the ground, swinging him over your shoulders and to the ground. Make the knee drop to the ground and the lifting action as swift as possible. (This is like the throwing action in Fig. 118, page 148.)

One other effective way to break the reverse chancery hold is as follows. As the assailant traps your head, reach up with both hands and catch hold of his arm as it goes under your chin and across your neck. Take as secure a hold as you can and lift your head up slightly so as to put some strength and tension into your neck muscles. Next sit down quickly and roll backwards, swinging your right foot up between the assailant's legs, not so much to kick him in the groin but to lift him from that area. As you roll backwards, maintain your tight grip and tension in your neck and push strongly up with your foot (Fig. 68). The action will send the assailant flying over your body head first towards the ground, something like the action of the throw on page 151.

If you keep a tight hold on the assailant's arm he will crash head first into the ground. If your hold is not tight enough he will almost certainly let go his grip as he feels himself falling forward.

Although I have said sit down and then roll backwards, the actions merge into one if done quickly. The more sudden the drop back the better, especially if it combines with the lift from the leg.

As you drop back, take care to keep your neck strong and pull down hard on the assailant's arm, otherwise you may hurt your neck.

Fig. 68

Hair grab

Both men and women may wear their hair long, which often leaves them open to attacks which begin by grabbing the hair. One of the first things to do with this type of attack is to relieve the pain felt on the head. Reach up and place your right hand over the assailant's hand (Fig. 69) and hold it as firmly as you can to your own scalp. This will relieve the pressure. Keeping a tight hold on the hand, pivot on your right foot round to your right so as to bring you facing the same direction as your assailant and bend forward. As you pivot and bend forward, the assailant's arm will be straightened. Depending on your relative heights, you can either crack your left elbow down on the back of the assailant's elbow (Fig. 70), smash your forearm into it, or simply push it with your hand down towards the floor. Striking the elbow may damage it and force him to let go of the hair. If you simply push the back of the elbow, the assailant will almost certainly let go as he feels his arm coming under control.

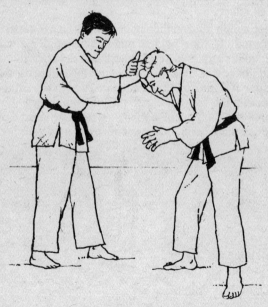

Fig. 69

Fig. 70

6

Ground Defences

It is a general rule of self defence to stay on your feet at all times. You are at a serious disadvantage if you are on the floor and your assailant is standing. If you are lying down, or even sitting, and trouble threatens, you must instantly get to your feet. However, in a one-to-one assault you may find yourself rolling on the ground with an assailant. The anthropologist who studied fighting in various cultures noted that after the initial flailing attack it was common for both parties to end up rolling around on the ground. It is therefore necessary to know what to do on the ground. There are a lot of moves that can be done, as any judo expert will attest to. Judo, incidentally, is probably the only martial art that seriously studies ground fighting from a combat point of view. Olympic wrestling has now moved completely away from the combat form that it once was.

The general rule on the ground is to get gravity on your side. Squash your assailant with your weight. When he is pinned to the floor he loses freedom of movement and must work against your weight, whereas you expend no energy at all when lying on him.

Do not lie directly on top of your man, but have about one half of your bodyweight off to one side, and hold tightly. If you lie directly on top he may find it easy to roll you off and reverse the positions. When on top, spread your weight out; when underneath, curl up in a ball and look for opportunities to roll him over, using your legs if possible. Once you can control the assailant from above you can then look for joint-lock and strangle possibilities.

When defending yourself on the ground, use your legs as much as possible to hold the assailant. The legs must be used like a second pair of arms.

Pinned on the ground

There are a number of ways in which you may be pinned to the floor. The two most likely ones are to have the assailant sitting across your stomach or kneeling between your legs, and attempting to strangle or batter you with his hands. There are a few counter-moves that can be made from underneath, but by far the best move is to reverse the situation by rolling your assailant over and swinging on top of him.

Defence One
Whether the assailant is between your legs or across your stomach, first trap one of his arms. Either catch hold of a wrist with your hand or catch his arm under your armpit. When you catch the wrist or arm, catch them on the same side as your own. That is to say use your right arm to catch his left one and *vice versa*. Next, reach up with your other arm and, sinking a clawlike hand into his face, bridge on to your shoulders (lifting your hips off the ground) and roll the assailant over to the side on which you have trapped his arm (Fig. 71).

Fig. 71

As he topples over, take care that the impetus of the move does not carry you right over him and underneath again. As you end up on top, either disengage quickly, or follow up with a quick punch to the head if across the stomach, or kneel on his testicles if between his legs.

It is essential to trap one of the assailant's arms. If you try to roll him over to the side and his arms are free, he will use them to stop the roll.

If the attacker should be pinning you to the ground but be kneeling or lying to one side of your body, bring your legs up and violently push him away. Then stand up quickly. In a serious situation you may then incapacitate the assailant by dropping both knees to his body or by jumping up and crashing both heels in.

Defence Two
Although the safest move in this situation is to roll the assailant off, lack of space may prevent you from doing this. You may be caught in a narrow passage, for example, where the assailant cannot roll to the side. In this case you must go for the sensitive areas of the assailant's anatomy as you lie underneath. If both of your hands are free, combine a poke in the throat with a sharp squeeze of his lower ribs (Fig. 72). Strongly extend your fingers, keeping them pinned tightly together, and push into the hollow below the Adam's Apple.

These two attacks may cause him to pull back sharply. If he is kneeling between your legs, use the opportunity to kick him away. If he is sitting astride your stomach try to pitch him head first over your

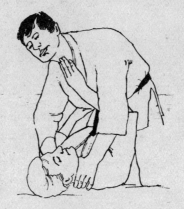

Fig. 72

head. To do this bring your feet close to your backside and bridge up violently with your hips. At the same time use both hands to catch him round the lower ribs and push him over your head. It is unlikely that he will go flying right over your head, but as he sprawls forward twist quickly round on to your stomach, bring your knees up and kneel, then straighten your legs. As you straighten the legs keep your head down and aim to slide the assailant down your back as you back out from between his legs.

Defence Three

One other common way to be pinned to the ground is when the assailant sits across your stomach and catches hold of both of your wrists and pins them to the floor by your head. He cannot actually do much to you as long as he has to hold both your wrists, but you are under control and must do something about it. The best way to deal with this situation is to try to unbalance him forwards. To do this push your wrists out sideways as far as they will go. This will cause him to widen his grip. Having widened the grip, bring your feet up close to your backside and suddenly bridge up, thrusting your hips high into the air. This should start to pitch him forward on to his face. He will probably let go of one of his arms to recover his balance. As he does so, use your free arm to push him off, either to one side or over your head.

Ground strangle

Defence One

When an assailant is attempting to strangle you on the ground but from the side of your body, you may need to do something more positive than push him away with your legs. Providing your legs are reasonably flexible it is possible to use them to catch the assailant in an arm-lock.

As the assailant's hands tighten around your neck, catch hold of both his wrists with your two hands. This not only relieves the pressure on the neck but helps the arm-lock as well. Roll on to your right hip (assuming the assailant is kneeling on your right side) and bring your right knee and shin across his chest, as if you were going to use it to push him away. Follow this by swinging your left foot right over the assailant's head to rest across his face, your foot almost on his left shoulder (Fig. 73). Having swung your left leg over his head, use it

Fig. 73

to push against his head and push him backwards to the ground. As he collapses to the ground you will find his straight right arm trapped between your legs. Keep it held firmly there and bring pressure on the elbow joint by lifting your hips off the ground and pulling his hand down towards your chest (as in Fig. 76, page 91). Do not attempt to lock both elbow joints, just concentrate on his right arm. In the final position you should be lying at a 90 degree angle to the assailant.

Defence Two

Sometimes the situation on the ground may be so pressing that you will have to do something drastic. When the assailant kneels beside you on the ground he is fairly vulnerable to two attacks to his sensitive spots.

The first is very simple but must be done with total resolution. Using your index and middle fingers, form them into a V-shape and prod both into the assailant's eyes. The eyes are very senstive and any threat to the general area is quickly reacted against. This is why the defence must be done quickly and resolutely. *This defence is only to be used in extreme cases.*

The other defence is to push or poke your index or middle finger into the cavity below the Adam's Apple. This defence can be used simply to push the assailant away, or to injure him, in which case the finger is poked violently into the cavity. Poking the neck is for extreme situations.

Defence Three

It may happen that your assailant attempts to strangle you as you lie on the ground, kneeling from your head end – that is to say, kneeling by your head facing your feet. This is not the most effective strangle position, but in the heat of the moment the assailant may not position himself too carefully.

As in many of the ground situations, the legs can be used to great effect. When the strangler's hands tighten around your neck, catch hold of both his wrists with both your hands. This relieves the pressure and helps the following move. Hold tight to the assailant's wrists and, using these to pull against, lift both legs up and swing them over towards the assailant's head. Depending on the size of the man and whether his arms are straight or bent, you may try different defences. If you have enough room, place both feet against the upper body, face or chest, and kick him away, taking care to release both wrists. Alternatively, try catching the strangler's head between your legs. As you catch the head, cross your feet over at the ankles and squeeze hard. Having caught the head in this way, swing your feet back the way they came, pulling the assailant head first over your body to the ground. Maintain the squeeze on the neck and see if you can apply a strangle.

Entangled arm-lock

If you manage to get your weight on the assailant, there are many opportunities to lock one of his arms as he thrashes around. This arm-lock is done as you lie across his chest. Catch hold of his wrist with your left hand and push his arm to the floor into an L-shaped position. Slide your right arm under his upper arm and grab your own left wrist. Press down heavily on his chest with yours and lift his elbow up by raising your right shoulder (Fig. 74). This will instantly cause pain to the elbow joint, which in this position is extremely weak. Either control the assailant by maintaining the hold, or incapacitate him by wrenching the joint.

This lock can also be done when you are lying on the ground with the assailant between your legs. Catch hold of his right wrist with your

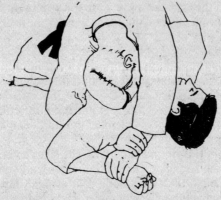

Fig. 74

left, reach up and over his shoulder, threading your right arm through the crook of his elbow to catch your own wrist. Hold the assailant tightly between your legs and pull his upper body down to the ground at your right side (Fig. 75). Bend the arm into an L-shape and push his hand up in the air. The lock will then take effect.

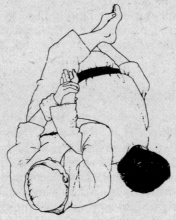

Fig. 75

Cross arm-lock

This arm-lock is especially popular among judo experts. Although the final position is always much the same, it can be applied successfully whatever position the opponent may be in. One of the best times to do it is after stumbling the assailant to the ground. As he lies at your feet catch hold of his right arm and pull it up straight, holding his wrist with both hands. Step over his head with your left foot, leave your right foot where it is, and sit down quickly by his right shoulder. As you sit down keep pulling on the assailant's wrist and trap his upper arm between your thighs. Lie back, keeping his arm straight between your legs (Fig. 76). To bring pressure on the elbow joint, pull his wrist down towards your chest and lift your hips up off the floor. You can either control him in that position or wrench the joint if necessary. When applying the final pressure make sure that the assailant's palm faces upwards and keep the arm held tight and straight. The final position in this lock is like a figure L. You must take care to lie at a 90 degree angle to the assailant.

Fig. 76

Armpit-lock

This is a very powerful arm-lock which can be applied against an assailant lying in a prone position. In the course of a fracas you may knock the assailant to the ground face down. This is a very disadvantageous position for him, so you must try to maintain it. As soon as he hits the ground sit beside him with your right hip and buttock on the ground, and bear your weight down across his lower back. Just by keeping your weight on that area you can keep him under control; however, he will almost certainly try to get up which will give you the opportunity for this arm-lock. As he tries to get up he will use his arms to push up from the ground. As soon as he puts his left arm to the

ground slide your right knee under it and push his arm out to the side
(Fig. 77). As you do this keep as much weight as possible bearing
down on him to keep him face down. Once you have pushed his arm
out to the side, catch hold of his wrist with both hands, straighten the
arm, then slide your right armpit down over his upper arm, taking
care all the time to keep him pinned face down.

Fig. 77

Fig. 78

In this position he is virtually powerless. To bring pressure on his elbow joint push down hard with your armpit on his upper arm and lever the lower part of his arm upwards (Fig. 78). Since his arm is already straight, very little movement is required to bring pressure on the joint. It is also possible to put on a shoulder-lock by levering the whole arm up and over his back.

Naked strangle

Defence One
This is an extremely effective ground move. The assailant is probably in the worst position he could be in – face down, flat on the ground. Getting the assailant there is not quite as difficult as it might look. In the course of a fracas he might stumble to the floor and while rising to his feet he might turn his back on you in an all-fours position. This often happens with an untrained man. Instantly, leap on his back, wrapping both legs around his body, your feet touching the inside of his thighs, and encircle his neck with your right hand (Fig. 79). Drive both your legs back and flatten the assailant to the floor keeping your legs hooked in position underneath. Clasp your hands together just under his left ear and, bearing down with your chest on the back of his head, pull both arms strongly up into his throat (Fig. 80). This strangle puts pressure on the windpipe, as opposed to the carotid artery in other strangles, and is extremely unpleasant. The assailant is virtually incapable of movement in this position, so you could simply hold him there.

Fig. 79

Fig. 80

Strangles are dangerous and only for real emergencies: see page 31 and the caution on strangles.

Defence Two

The previous strangle works very well because the assailant is trapped between your legs on the ground and cannot move: in this situation the hand position, though simple, works well. However, if the assailant's body is not controlled, the hand-hold is not quite strong enough. Against a sitting assailant, for example, the following variation is effective.

Approaching from the rear, quickly wrap the whole of your left arm round the assailant's neck. In this case his Adam's Apple should be almost in the crook of your elbow. Catch hold of your right forearm (or bicep) and fold your right arm round behind his head (Fig. 81). To

Fig. 81

bring pressure on the neck tighten the whole of your left arm and push forward with your right hand. This folded arm position is a very strong one which the assailant will find extremely difficult to break. No matter how much he throws his body around, hang on tight to the hold and he will soon be brought under control.

Use these defences only in emergencies: see page 31 and the caution on strangles.

Cross-arm strangle

The most effective strangles are those which make use of the assailant's clothing. Not only does the cloth give you a strong grip but the cloth itself bites into the neck with a rope-like effect. Often this type of strangle may not be possible if, for example, the assailant is wearing very light clothing such as a T-shirt. However, if the assailant is wearing an open-necked shirt or jacket of moderately strong material it will be fairly easy to apply a strangle.

As you are rolling around on the ground with your assailant, catch him as quickly as you can between your legs. This is a strong attacking position. Reach up with your right hand and catch hold of his collar, holding so that your fingers are inside the jacket and your thumb outside, just behind the assailant's ear. Reach up with your left hand and catch his collar on the other side with the same grip and hand position (Fig. 82). It is highly important that you hold on each side with your thumbs just behind the assailant's ears. If you hold with your hands in a more forward position the strangle will not be effective.

Fig. 82

To apply pressure, pull the assailant's head down towards your chest and pull your elbows out sideways from your body. Keep him trapped firmly between your legs all the while. This strangle will 'bite' almost immediately, bringing the assailant quickly under control. Take care to scissor the neck, not the chin.

When going for the hand-hold try not to reach up with both hands at the same time. Get one hand grip first, making sure that it is correctly positioned and firm, then quickly get the other one. This way the assailant may not immediately realise what you are trying to do.

Strangles can be dangerous and must only be used in real emergencies. See page 31 and the caution on strangles.

Rear collar strangle

By far the best method of strangling someone on the ground is from behind, using clothing. Either in the standing position or on the ground there are many opportunities to leap on someone's back and wrap yourself round his body. Locked in this position you are in almost total control and can easily effect a strangle. One such opportunity occurs when the assailant is kneeling on all fours. If you have knocked him to the ground he will nearly always go through this position in the process of getting back to his feet. As soon as you see him in this position, quickly sit astride his back and push your heels back between his thighs and grip firmly with the legs (Fig. 79, page 93). Do not put your feet to the ground to carry any of your weight. Reach round his neck with your left hand and catch hold of his collar just behind his right ear. As you do this, capsize yourself over to your right, taking the assailant with you. Having collapsed to the floor, cross your legs tightly around the assailant's stomach. Next, consolidate the strangle position by reaching *under* his right armpit to catch hold of his left lapel. This grip merely holds the assailant in position (Fig. 83).

To bring pressure on the neck, pull your left elbow back to produce a sort of wringing action on his neck and pull your right arm in the opposite direction. Hold tightly to the cloth as you do so. The strangle can be made more effective by squeezing the assailant between your legs and bending him backwards.

The key to this strangle is the positioning of your left hand: it must

Fig. 83

fit tightly round the neck and catch the cloth just behind the ear. All the other parts of the move merely serve to hold the assailant in position while the pressure is being applied.

Take care to use strangles only in extreme emergencies: see page 31 and the caution on strangles.

Leg strangle

The legs are much stronger than the arms. While a victim's arms may be much weaker than his attacker's arms, his or her legs are often more than strong enough if used in the right way. The legs can be used very effectively in a rough-and-tumble on the ground. Especially, they can be used to squeeze the neck or kidneys. If you have fallen to the ground and the attacker is between your legs reaching for your throat, lift your right leg and wrap it round his neck. Next, lift up your left leg and hook your right foot in the back of the knee, folding your left leg down (Fig. 84). This works well if you have also trapped one of the assailant's arms between your legs. Squeeze the thighs around the assailant's neck and force him to submit or be rendered unconscious.

This leg action does depend rather on the length of your legs and the size of the assailant. Provided there is not a great disparity in size, the leg action can be used around the assailant's trunk for a kidney squeeze. As the assailant kneels between your legs, encircle his trunk with them, fitting your right foot behind your left knee as above, and squeeze hard. If you can fit your foot behind your knee this will make an extremely strong hold that is very difficult to break. Pressure round the stomach will affect the kidneys which, if squeezed very hard, may rupture. This is a dangerous counter for the assailant and only to be used in a real emergency. If you cannot fit the foot behind the knee, just cross the legs at the ankles and squeeze.

Fig. 84

The legs may be used simply to scissor the neck without catching an arm as well. In this case, wrap your legs round the assailant's neck, crossing your legs over at the ankles, and exert pressure by straightening the legs. This may or may not strangle the assailant. It will provide a very strong lock around the neck which, if wrenched one way or the other, may be damaged. Damaging the neck is an extreme measure, never to be used lightly.

All the above moves are highly dangerous and must only be used in emergencies. See page 31 and the caution on strangling.

Leg-lock

The leg, being more powerfully muscled than the arm, does not give quite the same opportunities to lock. Whereas one can arm-lock an assailant just by using one's own arms, it is usually necessary to employ the whole of one's body to lock a leg. Nevertheless, once one is in the locking position it is just as effective as an arm-lock. Also, any damage that may be inflicted on a leg joint is usually more painful and serious, since the joints are much larger.

Defence One
The following leg-lock may be taken from a variety of positions. You may be simply thrashing around on the ground with an assailant and happen to catch a foot, or you may be lying on the ground with him standing beside you trying to kick you. Wherever you can catch the

foot your own legs are instantly brought into play. In this case it is described as a follow-on from one of your defensive moves. If you have knocked the assailant to the floor there is a good chance, if he is not stunned, that he will try to kick out at you. Step in quickly and catch his right leg and trap it under your right armpit. Lock your hands together and hold the leg firmly around the ankle. As soon as you have caught the leg, step over his left leg with your right and drop back to the ground. As you touch the ground, swing your right leg over his trapped leg (Fig. 85). To bring pressure on his ankle, wedge the bony part of your lower right forearm across the area between the heel and the bottom of the calf muscle, pull up against this and lean backwards.

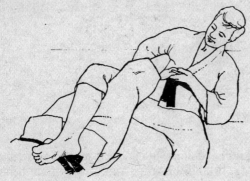

Fig. 85

Although Fig. 85 shows only the defender's right leg over the trapped leg, the lock can be made more effective by crossing your left leg over your right and using your whole body to pressure the leg.

Defence Two
In this leg-lock the assailant's knee is attacked. Damage to the knee joint may take several weeks to repair. Not only are leg-locks painful but they also disable the assailant to the extent that he cannot easily move around, run away or kick.

The lock that is described here is different from all the other locks described in the book. It does not work by twisting the joint or by over-straightening it. Instead, a wedge is inserted in the fold of the joint and the two ends are pushed towards each other, forcing the joint to separate.

Assuming that you have thrown the assailant face down to the ground, quickly move round to his legs and step across his left leg with your right. As you do this, catch hold of his left ankle, lift his lower leg up and sit down sliding your right ankle across the back of his knee. To bring pressure on the joint push the left foot forward so as to trap your own ankle snugly behind the knee (Fig. 86) and keep pushing the foot in towards the thigh. The pain does not always come on as quickly as with other types of joint-locks, but continue to push strongly and your assailant will eventually be brought under control.

Fig. 86

Another effective way of doing this leg-lock is to use the assailant's own foot as the wedge behind the knee. Approaching from behind, catch hold of the assailant's right foot, lift it up and swing it across, placing it behind his own left knee. At the same time catch hold of his left foot and fold it forwards so as to trap the right foot. Make sure that the right foot fits snugly at the back of the knee. Pressure on the joint is made as before, by pushing the foot down towards the buttocks.

The Soviet Sanbo wrestlers use leg-locks, and this is one of the common ways they catch their opponents.

Boston crab

The most dangerous joint-lock of all is the spine-lock: a damaged spine is either fatal or totally disabling. Although any joint-lock can be used to control an assailant (by bringing slight pressure on it) the spine-lock should be used only in the most serious of circumstances.

One of the most powerful spine-locks is the Boston crab, a move often seen in professional wrestling. Assuming that you have knocked your assailant to the floor, approach him from the leg end. When you see the opportunity, catch hold of both of his feet and trap them under each of your armpits. This will leave you standing fairly erect with the assailant's feet trapped under your armpits with his head and shoulders, face upwards, touching the floor.

Next twist round to your right and step over the assailant's body with your left leg so as to make a half-turn. As you do this, maintain a strong firm grip on his ankles and this will twist him over on to his face. The assailant will now be face down with you standing astride him, still with both legs trapped under your armpit.

So far little pressure will have been brought to bear on his spine. However, the lock is quickly applied by sitting down on his lower back and leaning backwards (Fig. 87). The assailant will have his face and upper body pressed to the ground and his legs and hips will be bent backwards over towards his head. To maintain pressure, make sure that you do not lose control of the feet. Otherwise he is totally under your control. The move can also be done from a single leg hold, as shown in Fig. 36.

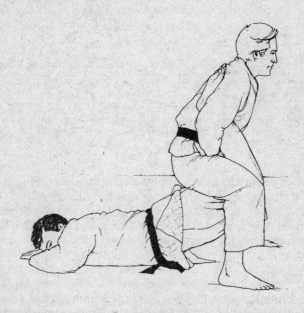

Fig. 87

Bringing down a standing assailant

When lying on the ground, you have the chance to knock down a standing assailant, especially if he stands too close. Seizing the opportunity when offered, hook your right instep around the heel of the assailant's leg and with your left foot push his knee back (Fig. 88), hooking his heel forward at the same time. As soon as he staggers over, leap to your feet. If you make this move quickly enough and kick at the knee, you may damage the knee.

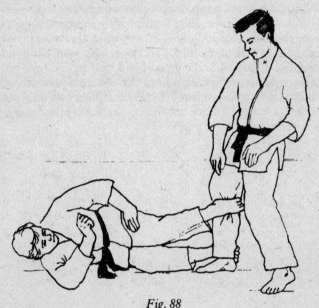

Fig. 88

Although essentially in a bad position, you may be able to put up a minimum defence against a standing assailant. Taking care to keep your feet towards the assailant, prop yourself up on both hands and use your feet to kick out at the assailant's knees and legs. This way you can keep him at bay for some time.

Covering up

It may happen that you will be knocked to the ground by one or more assailants who might then start kicking you. This is a very dangerous situation for you and one in which all attempts to minimise injury must be made.

Of course, all efforts must be made to keep off the ground; however, the average reaction when blows are raining down is to drop to the ground, even without being knocked there. If blows are raining down on you in the standing position, cover up like a boxer. Lift both arms, fists clenched, to about eye height, bringing your elbows together a few inches apart. Hunch forward and weave your upper body from side to side. The idea is not to intercept blows as you see them coming, but to put yourself in such a position that the minimum amount of damage can be done. By hunching forward you protect your stomach, and your arms are held in such a way as to take most of the blows that are aimed at your upper body. From this position lash out with hands and feet as appropriate.

To cover up on the ground, curl up in a ball, knees to chest and arms in the same position as the standing cover up. If possible, position yourself in a corner or against a wall so that your back is protected. This will considerably reduce the area that can be kicked. Take considerable care to protect your head with your arms. A kick to the head may stun you, leaving you vulnerable to further kicks to the head and body.

7

Defences Against Weapon Attacks

Never underestimate a knife-carrying assailant. The blade may be quite short, but it can do a great deal of damage either with a stab wound or a cut. Recall what it was like the last time you accidentally cut yourself – perhaps only slightly – and you will appreciate how much worse a deeper cut would be. Try to avoid this sort of confrontation if at all possible. If you have to deal with a knife attack, remember the general rules:

1. Show no resistance at all.
2. Keep talking, and look for opportunities to act.
3. Deal with the weapon before the man.
4. Move out of the line of the attack as you act.

When facing an assailant intent on using a weapon, have no scruples about using a weapon in defence. Anything that will put some distance between the blade and your skin may be used. The knife does not have to penetrate the main part of your body to be dangerous. A cut wrist can lose a lot of blood, and a cut at the back of your knee, for example, may put you out of action by slicing the sinews there.

One fairly common item which can be used as a defensive weapon is a chair. Keep jabbing the legs of the chair at the assailant and look for chances to knock him over and smash the weapon from his grasp. Alternatively, wrap a lot of cloth such as a coat or large towel round your left hand and forearm. If enough cloth is wrapped round the arm the knife will not easily cut or penetrate. Hold the left arm out in front as a sort of shield and look for chances to take the knife out of action.

When facing a knife, watch very closely how it is held. There are two main knife thrusts – low into the abdomen and high down to the chest. In each case the hand grip is different. If it is held point-down, pommel near the thumb, it will probably be used in a high downward stab. If it is held point towards you, pommel near the little finger, it will probably be used to thrust directly at the stomach.

The weapon itself may indicate what sort of an attack is likely. A wide blade with not much of a point may be used for cutting, in which case the blade will probably be held turned towards you. A long thin blade will probably be used for stabbing. A folding pocket knife may only be used for cutting since there is the danger that it may fold up if used for stabbing. If such a weapon clicks into position when unfolded it probably has a locking device to stop it folding. Look for these small details.

Check to see which hand the attacker holds the knife in. If you practise most of the following moves against a right-handed attack, do not get caught turning the wrong way against a left-hander.

An assailant may try to confuse you by flicking the knife from one hand to the other. Try to remember which hand the knife was held in before it was moved from hand to hand. This *may* indicate which side he is. Otherwise work on the probability that he is right-handed. If your assailant looks like an experienced knife-fighter, avoid him like the plague.

Defence One

As the attacker lunges forward, pivot on your left foot and swing the right side of your body and your foot back in a quarter-circle so as to take you out of the immediate path of the knife. At the same time, swing your left hand across to intercept the knife, pushing it further away from your body (Fig. 89). A split second later, crack the little finger edge of your right hand (karate-chop style) down on the attacker's lower forearm or wrist (Fig. 90). In doing this you are trying not only to knock the knife from his grasp but to injure his forearm. Instantly follow up this move with a right hook to the face.

If the blow to the forearm does not succeed in knocking the knife down, use whatever pause the pain in the arm might have caused, grasp his wrist with both hands and wrist-twist violently in an anti-clockwise direction. Maintain the pressure till the knife is dropped, then either pick up the knife yourself or knock it well out of reach.

Fig. 89

Fig. 90

If your right hook to the face knocks the assailant to the floor but he still manages to hold the knife, *instantly* follow up by catching the knife hand and applying a wrist-twist. Otherwise try to trample the weapon from his grasp or kick it away. Great care is needed. Be aware of the knife at all times.

Defence Two

This defence against a knife thrust to the stomach relies on catching the hand when it is fully extended in the thrust. If the assailant thrusts at your stomach with the full expectation of digging the knife in hard, and you move out of the way at the last second, his arm will stretch out to its maximum and he will lose his balance forward. At this moment it is not that difficult to catch the arm. However, mastery of the distance between yourself and the assailant is essential and requires some practice.

As the assailant approaches to within stabbing distance, stand squarely facing him in the Natural Stance. As he lunges forward, pivot on your left foot, swinging your right shoulder and side back and around in a quarter-circle. This will take you out of line of the knife. As the knife starts to go past your stomach, bring up your left hand

Fig. 91

and catch the assailant's right wrist in a pushing-down action (thumb towards your body, fingers on the outside). Having caught the wrist (Fig. 91) follow up first of all with a punch to his face with your right fist, then go for the wrist-twist.

Maintain your left-hand grip on his wrist, bring up your right hand from beneath, also catching the wrist, your fingers and thumb of each hand touching each other, then twist his wrist round and out in an anti-clockwise direction. This will topple him to the floor and make him drop the knife. If he is reluctant to drop the knife, keep twisting the wrist.

One of the advantages of showing no resistance and starting the defence in the Natural Stance is that the assailant may feel that you are totally defenceless and really lunge forward strongly. This then helps the defensive move considerably. On the other hand, if you raise your hands at the start of the confrontation this may make him slightly wary of going in hard, making it more difficult for you to catch the knife hand.

Downward stab

Defence One
Face the attacker in the Natural Stance. As the knife starts to swing down, move diagonally forward to the right side of the attacker, bringing up your right forearm to block the knife arm (Fig. 92). Having blocked the arm, instantly catch hold of his wrist with your right hand and pull the arm down, driving your left hand into the back of his elbow so as to straighten the whole arm. When straightening and pulling the arm down, pivot round a quarter-turn to your right and push the assailant face down to the ground (Fig. 18, page 33), keeping the pressure on his straight arm the whole time. Having brought him to the ground in this way, kneel on the triceps just above the elbow and force him to let go of the knife.

Apart from the initial blocking move, the aim in this defence is to use the impetus of the attacker and bring him to the ground in a single sweeping move, more or less following the path of the stab.

Defence Two
As with the previous defence against a downward stab, the assailant's arm is blocked just as he starts to plunge the knife down. To do this you must be keenly aware of the knife and leap in towards the assailant

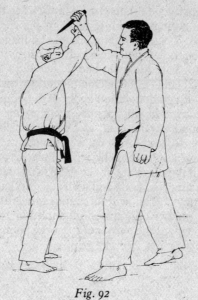

Fig. 92

the moment the knife starts to move.

As he approaches, knife in hand, adopt the Natural Stance and face him squarely. As he lifts the knife, leap quickly in towards him and block the downward sweep of his right wrist with your outer right wrist and push the arm back. To follow up, lift your left arm, snaking it under and behind his upper arm to catch your own right wrist. The arm position is virtually the same as the entangled arm-lock (Fig. 74, page 90). To make him release the knife, lever the knife hand backwards. As you lever it back the pain in his arm will force him off balance backwards and make him release the knife.

Virtually the same move can be made using your left arm to block, although it is not quite so effective.

Sideways stab

Apart from being stabbed in the back, which should not happen if your awareness is keen, the two most likely knife attacks are the straight thrust to the stomach and the downward stab to the chest. However, it is possible to meet an assailant who swings the knife in and around from the side. This is most likely when the assailant stands side-on to you, brings his knife hand to his chest and lashes out sideways at you. This sort of attack could be made by someone who overtakes you on the left side when walking, then lashes his right hand holding the knife back into your body.

The assailant stands right side on to you clutching the knife in his right hand. At this point note how he holds the weapon. If the pommel is near his little finger he will not make a sideways sweep with it. As his arm swings round towards you, block his right lower forearm with your right lower forearm. As soon as you block the swing, twist your right hand round so as to catch his wrist. Push his wrist in towards his body so as to lift the elbow and make the arm into an L-shape. Pull the wrist back towards your body and with your left hand push his elbow forwards and down. This will force him forwards and down to the ground and as you twist the arm more, force him to release the knife. Take care throughout the move not to let the point of the knife touch you. Catch his wrist in a vice-like grip.

Fig. 93

Upwards stab

In one other form of knife attack the assailant swings the knife up and under from below, aiming for the lower abdomen.

As the assailant swings the knife up, pull your hips back and thrust both hands down, right over left so that your arms form a cross-block. This block is virtually the same as the cross-block to the front kick (Fig. 37, page 49). Having blocked the upward thrust of the knife, swing your left hand out towards your left side and catch hold of the assailant's upper right arm with your right hand (Fig. 93). Pull the upper arm forward and push the arm into an L-shape. As you do this, pivot on your left foot round to your right so as to bring you round the assailant's side. This will bend him forwards with his knife arm trapped in the crook of your left arm (Fig. 94). Forward pressure will cause pain to the arm, making him release the knife. If he does not, keep the arm securely trapped, and prise the knife out of his grasp with your left hand. Depending on how far down the assailant is forced, you may be able to knee him in the face with your right knee, or chop the back of his neck with your right hand.

Fig. 94

Broken bottle in face

Since a lot of violence occurs in social situations where glasses and bottles are much in evidence, it is not unusual to find them used as weapons. In particular, a broken bottle is often used to jab at the face. An attacker will pick up a bottle, break the bottom off and use the jagged end to thrust at his victim's face.

Unlike a knife which has a point and a cutting edge, the broken bottle has a series of sharp points, thus while the points must be avoided the lower end of the bottle near the hand can be safely grasped.

When the broken bottle is used to jab straight at the face, the basic defensive move is to parry the attacker's right wrist with your left hand, swinging your body and head off the line as you do so. Having parried the thrust, use both hands to clasp the assailant's right hand and wrist-twist his hand in an anti-clockwise direction. This will force him to release the bottle and drop him to the ground. The parrying action is the same as that in Fig. 22 (page 37) and the wrist action is the same as that in Fig. 93 and Fig. 97.

Disarming an assailant

Most of the defences against a knife involve catching the arm in some sort of joint-lock, forcing the assailant face down to the floor, then continuing the pressure against the joint to make him release the knife. With joint-locks of this kind, much depends on how stiff the joint is. If it is of average stiffness the slightest twist will often cause such pain that the knife is dropped immediately. However, some people are very loose jointed and twisting the joints brings no immediate reaction. You may force them to the ground but they may hang on to the knife. In this case it helps to know one or two tricks for prising the knife from their grasp. Assuming that you have brought the assailant face down to the ground and have him under control, try the following methods of disarming him.

1 Force the clenched knuckles in towards the inside wrist (palm inwards). This will automatically open the hand. This can sometimes be done by placing the knife-holding hand in a press-up position (knuckles on the floor) and bearing down on it so that the hand folds inwards, back of the hand flat to the floor.

2 Force the thumb side of the hand to the floor. Assume that the assailant is lying on his front, knife arm out to the side, point sticking up. Bear down on both his body and arm then press his knife hand down and round so that the thumb is pushed down to the ground (palm uppermost).

3 Kneel on the nerve spot above the elbow where the sinews of the triceps insert into the bone. This is best done on a straight arm.

Combine all of these moves with a command to the assailant to drop the knife. Other than the above, you might try brute force such as trampling on the hand or banging it hard on the ground. Whatever you do, never lose control of the knife arm.

Having prised the knife from the assailant's hand, either throw it right away or maintain possession. Only keep hold of the weapon, however, if you are confident that you can stop the assailant regaining possession.

Front hold-up

In this and the next move the assailant has a hand-gun. As with a knife, moves against a gun are assumed to be only for use in the last resort. The major difference between self-defence moves against a knife and a gun is that whereas the edge or point of the knife must be totally avoided, a gun may be safely grasped provided it is not pointing at you. Hand-guns vary, but with a revolver for example, grasping the revolving chamber will stop the action of the gun, and with some automatics stopping the ejector movement will limit the weapon to one shot. Those who may have to deal with armed assailants, such as the police or security forces, must study the various weapons.

If someone wants to shoot you, he will do so without warning. If he wants to detain you for some purpose you have the chance to disarm him provided he is standing close enough. It is not impossible to disarm someone since it is not the bullet that has to be out-speeded but the assailant's eye-brain-finger reaction, which may be quite slow. Try practising some of these moves against a toy pistol that makes a bang and you will see how it can be out-speeded. Remember the general rules for dealing with a gun:

1 Do not make a move unless you can reach the gun.
2 Show no resistance at all.

3 Keep talking, look the assailant in the eye and look for a chance to act.

4 When you see your chance, move like lightning.

If an assailant approaches and aims a gun at your stomach, raise your hands whether he tells you to do so or not. Provided he is close enough, make the following move.

Pivoting on the left foot, swing your right foot and side back and round in a quarter-circle. At the same time bring your left hand sharply down and push the hand and the gun away from you, then catch hold of the hand. Instantly swing your right hand in from underneath and catch hold of the barrel (do not cover the end) as well (Fig. 95). Next, twist the barrel of the gun so that it points up in the air (Fig. 97) and keep twisting down and round in an anti-clockwise direction, taking care that the barrel is not pointing at you at any time. Keep twisting till the weapon is wrenched from the assailant's grasp.

Fig. 95

Rear hold-up

The grip on the gun and eventual disarming action are the same as for the previous move. However, they have to combine with a very swift spin round.

Having realised that someone is close behind you with a gun, raise your hands. It is marginally easier to bring your hands down quickly than it is to raise them when going for the gun.

When you decide to go for it, spin swiftly round to your right, on your right foot, bringing your right arm down in a karate-chop movement (Fig. 96). The swift action of the arm will push the assailant's gun hand aside and bring you close to him. Grab the hand and gun as before, left hand on top, right hand underneath, thumbs almost touching, and twist the barrel up to the sky, then down and round (Fig. 97) in an anti-clockwise direction until it is wrested from his grasp.

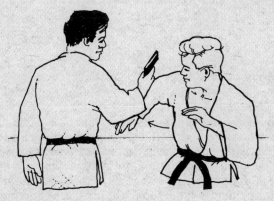

Fig. 96

Should the assailant be prodding the gun in your back with his left hand, spin round, bringing the arm down in a chopping movement and catch hold as before. However, instead of twisting the gun hand, push the barrel back towards his forearm, that is, in the direction his hand would have to go if his knuckles were forced back to touch the arm. You may not realise which hand was used to prod you in the back until you have spun round. Just be ready to make the different disarming actions.

Fig. 97

Stick blow

Defence One

Indoors or outdoors, there are many stick-like objects that an assailant can grab to attack you with. If heavy enough and wielded properly, such objects can be exceedingly dangerous. Against a stick-carrying assailant there are two safe areas – just beyond the reach of the stick and close in. As the assailant swings his weapon you must either jump out of reach or jump in close. Jumping in close can be done as the stick is lifted or after it has swung past. Merely jumping out of reach will prolong the encounter, so at some point when the time is right the assailant has to be closed with. Whichever moment is chosen to leap in, it must be done resolutely. When it is time to move, go in hard and fast.

Probably the best time to deal with a stick-blow is in the early stages, just as it is being lifted high. As the assailant lifts his right arm to bring the stick down, move in close, blocking the downward action of his arm with your left wrist and forearm on his wrist. Instantly, use your left hand to catch hold of the arm and with your right hand catch the assailant's throat. Swing your right leg behind the assailant's right knee and hook his leg forwards (Fig. 98). As you hook the leg away, push strongly into his throat with your right hand and dash him to the floor.

Fig. 98

The most important part of the whole defensive move is the speed with which you leap in. One Japanese Ju-jitsu school describes the action poetically as like diving under an enormous wave that is just about to smash you down.

Defence Two
As the assailant raises the stick, step in close to him and block the downward sweep of the stick-holding arm with your left outer wrist and lower forearm. Block fairly close to his wrist so as not to allow the stick to fold down on to your head. Push the arm backwards and swing your right arm under and behind his upper arm to catch your own left wrist (Fig. 99). Having caught your own wrist, lever his arm backwards until he drops the stick. As you lever his arm backwards take care to keep his arm in a rough L-shape.

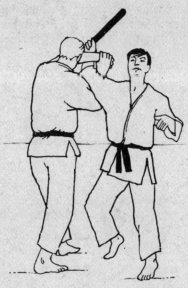

Fig. 99

The stick is not to be feared except when it is swinging down, so the crucial phase of the defence is at the very beginning. The moment the assailant lifts the stick to strike, you must step in very quickly and make the block. Practise stepping in smoothly and quickly, taking care that you start at just the right distance away. If you start too far away you will not be able to cross the gap in time.

Defence Three
As with many other types of attack the cross-arm block serves equally well against a stick attack. As the assailant lifts his stick arm, step in close with your left foot and punch both arms upwards so as to cross over and intercept the assailant's wrist in a V-shape (Fig. 100). Do not simply present the cross-arm position to the wrist, but punch up strongly so as to meet the force of the blow. Once the blow has been intercepted and stopped there is a choice of follow-on moves:

1 Catch hold of the assailant's wrist with your left hand, pull it sideways to the left and catch hold of his throat with your right hand. Follow up by throwing him to the ground, with your right leg hooking away his right leg, as in Fig. 98.

Fig. 100

2 Catch hold of his wrist, again with your left hand, and pull it to the side. At the same time, keeping your right hand in a fist, chop it down into the side of the assailant's neck or on the collar-bone.

3 Catch hold of his wrist with your right hand, pulling his arm down and round to your right side and pushing strongly into the back of his elbow to straighten the arm out. Continue the move by pushing into the elbow and forcing him to the ground, face down. The move is similar to the knife defence in Fig. 92 (page 109).

Defence Four

The longer the stick the assailant carries, the further away you must stand to be out of range. On the other hand, if he carries a fairly short, cosh-like stick the closer you can come, giving you the opportunity to use your feet.

Against a cosh attack, first of all stand squarely facing your assailant in the Natural Stance. As he gets to within kicking distance, lift your arms up as if going to the Ready Stance but swing them round to your left, pivoting on your left foot and spinning the whole body round as well. The spin should take you round somewhere between a quarter- and a half-turn to the left.

Look over your right shoulder, drop your upper body down and kick back with your right foot into the assailant's knee (Fig. 101). The kick is done, like all kicks, by lifting the knee and folding the leg, then lashing out backwards in a mule-like kick. When practising this kick, really stretch the leg as far as it will go. This will require good balance, which can be acquired with practice. Having made the kick, quickly pull your foot back and take care not to turn your back fully to the assailant. Keep your eye on him throughout the move and follow up with another kick if necessary. The spin-and-kick combination requires some dexterity but it is well worth practising. Turning your back on the assailant can often give him the impression that you are afraid and backing down. A sudden backwards kick can often catch him unawares.

Fig. 101

Garotte defence

The garotte in an attack is every bit as lethal as a knife or a stick. It must not be underestimated. In this attack the assailant whips a length of rope or wire around your neck and proceeds to strangle you with it. The threat to the neck is so immediate that not a second must be lost in dealing with it. Your immediate reaction to having a rope tightened round your neck is to try to dig the fingers under it to relieve the pressure. However, if the rope is thin or biting strongly into your neck this may not be possible and you will be wasting vital seconds. Instead, reach up behind your neck, grab what rope you can and then hurl yourself to the floor. In this way you hope to shatter completely the assailant's grip and his balance. This is not an elegant defence move but you will appreciate its effectiveness when your training partner tightens a piece of rope round your neck. There is little else to do when the rope is biting in.

8

Stick Techniques

There are two reasons for learning how to wield a stick properly. The first is that you may be able to find a stick-like object with which to defend yourself when attacked by several assailants, or one carrying a knife. Secondly, a walking stick may be carried quite legitimately, especially by the elderly, without your being detained by the police for carrying an 'offensive weapon'. A youngster of course may have trouble convincing the police that he needs a stick, but an older person may well carry one, when out at night or in dangerous places, without attracting attention. When choosing a stick with self-defence purposes in mind, select a fairly stout one; a light stick has limited uses. If possible, find one that does not have a curved handle.

If you are attacked by an armed assailant or by several assailants, any stick-like object may be used to defend yourself successfully. Either in the home or outdoors you may be able to find something suitable, but it is necessary to know how to use it. You may not have much choice in the matter but the object you choose should be about four feet long and fairly heavy. If it is too short you will not have much range, and if too long or heavy it will be unwieldy. A stout walking stick would be suitable, though the average stick is on the light side (see also page 130, Use of umbrella). The use of a weapon such as a stick is not for casual purposes: the police may decide it is an offensive weapon. Only use such weapons in extreme emergencies.

Stick stance

Stance with a stick is just as important as stance without one. Faced with the threat of violence, the stick must not just dangle limply in your hand, or be raised half-heartedly. The stick must be held resolutely in a position from which you can defend or counter-attack with maximum effect. The stick stance shows that you accept the possibility of violence and are ready to deal with it.

To adopt the Stick Ready Stance, hold the stick diagonally in front of your body between your two hands, left hand palm uppermost, right hand palm down. Have your feet about shoulder-width apart, with the left foot and side to the front (Fig. 102). When you hold the stick, make sure you grasp it with all of your fingers. They do not have to be digging into the wood, but each must firmly play its part.

Fig. 102

Practise adopting the Ready Stance with the stick from a normal walking stick hold. With a little practice you will be able to flick the stick up quite smoothly.

From the Ready Stance practise the following blocking moves. Raise the stick, holding it parallel to the ground, just above your head. Imagine you are blocking a stick crashing down on your head. Next, still keeping it parallel to the ground, bring it down to groin height as if blocking a kick to the groin. Next, holding it vertically, swing it out to your left side and then to your right side. In each case imagine you are blocking a stick swinging round to hit your side. The four moves, as it were, fill in the four sides of an imaginary square in front of your body.

Also practise the above in the reverse stance, which is to say with the right foot and side forward and your right hand palm uppermost, left hand palm down.

Finally, one offensive move can be done from the Ready Stance. Drive the stick forward and up, aiming the middle of it for an assailant's throat. As you do so, lunge forward with the left foot. Either aim the middle of the stick for the throat or try to lift the assailant's chin. The move has to be done quickly since there is the danger that the assailant may catch hold of the stick.

Stomach jab

A stick can be used very effectively for jabbing as well as for hitting. When using the stick for jabbing, both ends of the stick can be used. The following move illustrates how the stick can be used against two assailants.

Assume two assailants confront you and are standing a few feet apart. Adopt the Ready Stance with the stick. When the opportunity presents itself, lunge forward with your left foot and jab the stick into the stomach or solar plexus of the assailant on your left. Get your weight behind the stick. Instantly adjust your position as necessary and jab the other end of the stick back into the other assailant's stomach (Fig. 103). Having made both strikes, move through both assailants to a position about three feet away. The danger with any stick technique is that an assailant may manage to catch hold of the stick. Therefore you must make your moves suddenly, then move quickly out of range, either back to your original position or beyond the assailants.

The stomach jab can be practised from the Ready Stance against a single assailant. When you confront the assailant in the Stick Ready Stance there is a good chance he will try to grab the stick. Get your training partner to move as if grabbing the stick, then drop the left end of the stick down, lunge forward with the left foot, dropping your body fairly low, and jab the end of the stick into the stomach under his outstretched arms. Instantly recover your position.

Fig. 103

End swing

One other type of strike with a stick, which is not strictly a straight jab or a blow, is to push one end of the stick into the assailant's body or face using the force of your arms.

Confront your assailant, holding the stick in the Ready Stance, left foot and side forward. Step forward with your right foot and, at the same time, drive your right arm forward swinging the lower end of the stick up into the assailant's solar plexus (Fig. 104). Alternatively, step forward and drive the end of the stick into the assailant's jaw.

The move can be done by swinging the higher end of the stick into the assailant's face, though it is not so effective. To be able to use both ends of the stick effectively it will be necessary to change grip, right hand palm uppermost, left hand palm down, with the right hand end higher than the left. Being able to switch the grip around like this is very useful. The assailant may not always be standing in the right position for the left side forward Ready Stance.

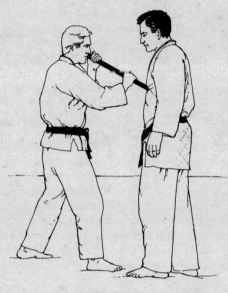

Fig. 104

One good way to practise this type of stick blow with a training partner is to move forward slowly as he retreats, swinging first the right-hand end of the stick into his body, then the left, then the right again into the jaw and finally the left into the jaw. Each blow is made with your foot stepping forward on the same side as the connecting end of the stick.

With a heavy stick-like object this type of move is very effective. The army use it in bayonet fighting, when the heel of the rifle butt is cracked up after the use of the bayonet, or after parrying the enemy's bayonet.

Knee and arm strike

Armed with a stout stick, there is no great problem concerning where to hit. Almost anywhere will hurt the assailant. The general rule with the stick, however, is to strike the bones rather than the flesh, as blows struck on the bony areas are excruciatingly painful. Starting from the bottom, the targets are therefore: ankles, shins, knees, hips, wrists, elbows and shoulders. Other targets are the upper arm between the shoulder and the elbow and, of course, the head. The danger with attacking the head is that the assailant may die if the blow is too hard and a softer blow may be ineffective. Since it is difficult to judge and vary the force of a blow to the head, only attack this area if you have to.

This next move with the stick is made with two hands. A double grip on a stick generates much more power. In most cases a stout stick will be too heavy to wield with one hand.

From the Ready Stance, lift the stick high with your right hand and transfer your left hand to grip directly beneath the right. From this high position you have a choice. Either crack the stick down and round on the assailant's left shoulder or upper arm, or swing it down and round in a bigger circle and crack it across the side of his left knee (Fig. 105). By raising the stick high in the first place you can often make the assailant lift his arms to protect his head and this then leaves his knees open to attack. Practise moving from the Ready Stance into the high position and then into the blow in one smooth movement,

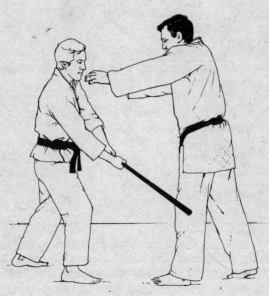

Fig. 105

alternating between a high strike and a low strike. It is fairly easy to make the knee strike but you must convince the assailant that you are going for the head first.

Wrist strike

The stick is an ideal weapon to use against a knife since its length keeps you well out of range of the blade. When facing a knife, the target to aim for is the wrist or the elbow of the assailant. A sharp crack in either of these places will put the arm out of action. Which target you go for depends on how the assailant wields the knife. If he lifts the knife up for a high downward stab he will expose his elbow, in which case change your grip on the stick, right hand palm uppermost, left palm down, right end of the stick high, and crack the stick across his uplifted arm, aiming for his elbow or any part of the forearm down to the wrist (Fig. 106). To get a good swing at his elbow you may need to step out to your left slightly.

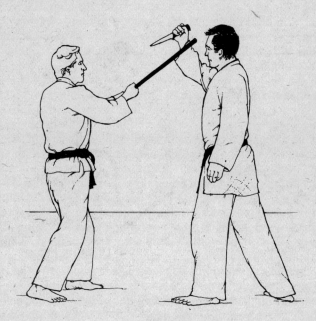

Fig. 106

If the assailant tries to thrust the knife into your stomach, you have more of a problem, since his wrist is not such an easy target. Against this sort of attack, switch your grip on the stick as with the previous defence, step wide to your left side (assuming a right-handed knife attack) and crack the end of the stick down across the assailant's wrist or lower forearm. As you make the blow to the wrist, slide your right hand down the stick to meet your left.

When you make these stick defences against a knife, take care not to let the assailant get too close. You will need some distance to get a good swing with the stick.

A stick shorter than a walking stick can be used with more effect against a knife provided it is weighty enough and that you can swing it in one hand. In this case use it exactly as above.

The big stick

There is an ancient story told of a simple farmer who accidentally insulted a Japanese warrior. The warrior immediately challenged the farmer to a duel the following day at dawn. The warrior was of course a highly trained swordsman and the farmer knew he stood no chance whatsoever. However, the farmer went to get advice from a retired master-swordsman who lived nearby. 'The first thing you must realise,' he was told, 'is that tomorrow you will die. Make your final arrangements. Next, you must face your death in this way. Hold the sword in both hands high above your head and look straight at your opponent. Make no move to fence with him, just bring your sword down with all your might the moment he is about to pierce or slice you – not a second before. Meditate all night on your death!'

The farmer did as he was told and the next morning faced the warrior, sword held high and motionless. The warrior advanced and attempted to draw the farmer with some feinting moves, but the farmer remained motionless. Again the warrior edged closer, preparing himself for a lunge, but then withdrew again. After two more similar self-aborted moves the warrior withdrew, sheathed his sword, bowed and left. The warrior had realised that whatever final move he made, the farmer's sword would come crashing down on him and both would die.

This story is applicable to the stick. When in dire straights, hold the stick high above your head and resolve to smash it down on your attacker's head come what may. Do not be put off by small movements, just wait for that split second when he is completely within range. The point about the move is that it must be totally resolute and powerful. The attacker will not approach if he senses that resolution.

Practise the move on a suitably placed cushion. You will be amazed how much force you can generate after a few practice strokes.

Although in the story it was certain death for both farmer and warrior if both used their swords, this of course does not apply with the stick, especially if the assailant is unarmed or carries a shorter weapon such as a knife.

Use of umbrella

The umbrella may well be the only stick-like object that you may have at hand in a violent situation. Compared with a stout stick the umbrella has limited uses. It is likely to be quite light and of flimsy construction with only one useful feature – a sharp point. To be used effectively, the point must be used to stab at the exposed parts of the body such as the face, or the stomach if the attacker is not wearing too much clothing. Hold it in the same way as the Stick Ready Stance and lunge forward with it using both hands, taking care not to get the umbrella caught. Used in this way, it will create a nasty wound and should only be used in *real emergencies*.

The stabbing action with the umbrella may be used to keep an assailant at bay while you try to raise help. It can also be used to hit an assailant with but, since most umbrellas are quite light, this may be of little use. Depending on the circumstances, use the umbrella in a barrage of blows to put the assailant on the defensive, then use the point.

The stick techniques described above are simple and few in number. If you acquire a stick, practise as often as you can so as to get the feel of it. Learn to slide it through your fingers smoothly and easily and to twirl it around. With practice the stick will become like a living extension of your arm.

9

Offensive and Miscellaneous Techniques

There are a number of reasons for learning offensive as opposed to defensive moves. When attack is certain and imminent it is better for you to move first. Also one often has to be able to follow up a defensive move with an offensive one. There is never certainty that your first defensive move will succeed. Against two or more assailants you cannot wait for each one to attack first, but must deal with all as abruptly as you can. This chapter also includes a few miscellaneous techniques which are neither offensive or defensive, but which are necessary in the self-defence situation.

Distraction

There is a poetic Japanese name for this type of technique. It is *Kasumi-waza* and means literally 'mist technique'. Probably the nearest English equivalent would be smoke-screen techniques.

It is quite difficult for the untrained person to make a successful offensive move. In the same way that you can often sense that someone is about to hit you, it is not difficult for him to detect the small signs that give away your intentions. What is often required is a spring-board for one's main attack. A light distraction serves not only to distract the assailant but to give you that spring-board.

One simple type of distraction is to throw something in the assailant's face. Anything that you may have in your pocket such as coins, a bunch of keys, a handkerchief or pens will do. As casually as possible, grasp the object, then dash it into the assailant's face. If close enough you can also spit in the assailant's face. Follow up immediately with your avoidance, control or incapacitation technique.

Throwing something in the face is probably the best trick, but there are alternative distraction techniques. You can pretend to throw something, or talk to an imaginary person behind the assailant, or scream out 'Fire!'. Whispering to the assailant will often cause him to listen intently to what you are saying, and a wagging finger has a hypnotic effect. Simply pointing to one side with your finger will often make the assailant's eyes shift for a second.

Eye-flick

With this technique the aim is to make the eyes water for a while, giving you time to get away. Most people will have experienced a slight knock in the eye which causes intense watering and the inability to look out of either eye for a few minutes. One way to achieve this effect in a self-defence situation is to flick the fingers of one hand across the general area of the eyes.

Make the hand as floppy as possible, especially the fingers, and flick the backs (nail side) of the fingers across the eye area. By keeping the fingers floppy they will spread out and move into the indentations.

The whole move must be done lightly, but fast. To get some idea of the movement practise flicking the fingers of one hand into the palm of your other hand. Remember, the aim is not to jab the fingers into the eyes but to flick lightly across them.

Rabbit chop

The name of this move comes from the way rabbits' necks are broken. The karate name for the hand position is Te-gatana or Shuto, both of which mean 'hand-sword'. The action is very much like bringing a sword down on the back of someone's neck, except that it is done with the edge of the hand.

This is a lethal move. There is no way that you can do it softly to cause temporary discomfort. When it is done hard it breaks the neck. Thus the move is only to be used when fighting for your life.

The action of the move is simple. You crack the little finger edge of your hand across the back of the assailant's neck. When your hand makes contact, it is the part of your hand near to the bony projection by the wrist that does so, not the part by the base of the little finger.

The only problem is getting the assailant's neck in the right position. If he stands up straight it is difficult to hit correctly. The best chance is when he is bending forward and you are to one side. The assailant may bend forward in the course of an encounter or you may be able to pull his head down. If the assailant has long hair this makes it easy to pull the head down. When the head is in position, tense the hand and crack it down across the back of the assailant's neck. The more relaxed the neck is, the better.

Head butt

Defences against this move are often taught (see page 64) since it is a common form of attack. It is of course a useful move in its own right, and works well for close-quarter encounters and for those shorter than their assailant. Since it has to be done at close quarters a certain amount of guile and trickery must be used to get within striking range. Alternatively you may end up quite close to the assailant in the course of an encounter.

When close enough, catch hold of both of the assailant's lapels. Pull him in sharply towards you and at the same time lower your head and

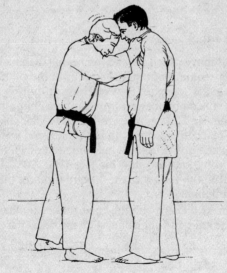

Fig. 107

butt the top of it, just above the hair line, into the assailant's nose (Fig. 107). This move can also be made if the assailant is standing at your side. Without catching hold, simply flick the top of your head into his face. Take care that you do not crack the side of your face into his.

Stomach butt

This is another move that can be used by someone considerably shorter than his assailant. At one time it was a move much depicted in children's comics when the tiny hero had to deal with an adult thug. It is a deceptive move which seems harmless enough not to bother about. In fact it can easily wind your assailant, or worse.

Lower your head quickly and with a short lunge drive the top of it into the assailant's stomach. It only takes a few practice runs at a heavy punch bag to make it into an effective surprise move. It is a great advantage to be a good deal shorter than your assailant since your head does not have so far to travel. When making the move take care not to signal your intentions. Drop the head down and ram it into the stomach in one smooth, fast move.

Knee in the face

This is a vicious move which depends on having the assailant's head in range. This may come about quite naturally in the course of a fracas, or you can create the opportunity by reaching up quickly and dragging his head down; the more unawares you can catch him, the better.

Assuming the assailant has thrown a punch to your head, which you have stopped, reach up quickly with both hands and violently pull his head forwards and down. As you pull the head down to about waist height, drive your knee up into his face (Fig. 108). Combine the downward pull on the head with the upward thrust of the knee so that both meet in full flight.

When you make contact with the knee, make sure that it is with the bony part of the knee and not half way up the fleshy part of the thigh.

Fig. 108

Immobilisation

Technique One

The purpose of this move is to immobilise the assailant. You may want to hold him helpless till the police come or other help arrives or try to subdue or bind him.

The actual immobilisation position is simple. The assailant is held face down on the ground. You hold one of his arms jammed up his back and kneel heavily down on the area between his mid-shoulder-blades and neck, facing his feet (Fig. 109).

Many of the moves illustrated in this book knock the assailant to the floor face down. Whichever way he manages to land on his face, first pin him to the ground by kneeling from his head end down on the spine between his neck and shoulder-blades. This will more or less immobilise him but, to make absolutely sure, catch one of his arms as he thrashes around and jam it up his back.

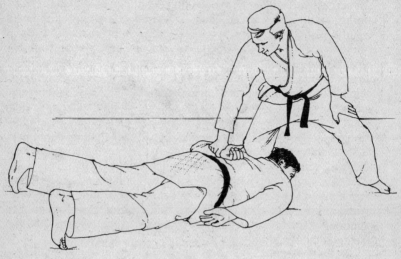

Fig. 109

Technique Two

Another way to hold someone face down helpless on the ground is to approach him from the feet end and sit down across his lower back, knees on the ground, feet alongside the body.

If this is done quickly enough it is usually possible to catch hold of first one arm at the wrist, and then the other, and lever them backwards straight up in the air. The combined pressure of the assailant's hands being pushed in towards each other and the straight arms being forced forwards causes sufficient pain on the assailant's shoulders to immobilise him totally.

It may not always be possible to take both arms more or less at the same time. However, if one arm is taken and levered up backwards, the assailant can be sufficiently controlled for the defendant to watch for opportunities to take the other arm. The pain in one shoulder will be enough to distract him.

Technique Three

It may happen that you fall to the ground on top of your assailant who lands on his back, in which case you may need to immobilise him as he lies face up.

Sit across the assailant's stomach, knees on the ground, lower legs running back alongside the body. In this position he will almost certainly reach up with his arms either to grab your throat or clothing. As he does this, slide forward, keeping your knees pressed tightly against his body until you are almost sitting astride his throat with both arms trapped between your two knees. Press your knees strongly together, forcing the assailant's arms to cross over. As they cross over, catch hold of both wrists and pull the forward one back and push the nearest one forwards. This will entangle both his elbows, putting a joint-lock on both. When you are in position the feeling is very much like steering a bicycle. Turning to the left or right, depending on which way his arms are crossed over, will lock the joints.

The only danger to watch in this position is that the assailant may lift up both his legs and try to swing them over your head to trap you between them and roll you backwards. If he does so, lean forward out of range. At the same time increase pressure on the elbows and this will stop him dead.

Come-along hold

The purpose of this technique is to move somebody under control from one place to another. You may want to remove somebody from your property or drag him to where you can get help. It is the sort of technique used by the police when arresting someone.

Technique One
Catch hold of the assailant's left wrist in a cross-grip. Pull his arm across your body, stepping to his left side as you do so. Thread your right arm over the top and round his biceps, under his elbow, and catch hold of your own left wrist. As you thread your right arm round, keep the assailant's arm straight and twist it so that his palm is facing outwards. Once you have caught your own wrist (or your own clothing) make sure that your right arm encircles the assailant's upper arm, and that the white inside of his elbow is fully exposed and facing to the front (Fig. 110). With this powerful hold, bring pressure on to the elbow by straightening the arm and, maintaining that pressure, walk him along to wherever you wish to take him. When the pressure is properly on, the assailant will probably rise up on to his toes with the pain. Provided you keep him in that position he will be unable to make any counter-move.

Fig. 110

The technique has to be made quickly before the assailant has time
to tense his arm. A light blow to the face may distract him sufficiently
for you to do this.

Technique Two

This come-along-hold is most effective against an assailant wearing
fairly thick clothing on the upper body. Without such clothing it does
not work.

Face the assailant and catch hold of his wrist in a cross-grip – your
left hand catching his left wrist. Pull his left wrist towards your left
hip, which will bring him sideways-on to you, and reach under his left
armpit from the rear with your right arm to catch his right-side lapel
high up on the chest. As you catch hold of the lapel, straighten and
twist his left arm in an anti-clockwise direction so that the palm of his
hand faces out away from his body, and straighten your right arm.
This will bring pressure on the assailant's left elbow which can be
increased by pushing his left wrist in towards your stomach.

When you catch the lapel, take care to hold high up near the
collar-bone with your fingers inside and the thumb outside, and keep
his arm straight all the time.

Once you are able to apply pressure to the elbow joint you will be able to walk the assailant on tip-toe to wherever you want.

Technique Three

The two previous come-along holds work by applying pressure on the assailant's elbow joint. This one works by applying pressure on his wrist.

It is probably best applied by approaching the assailant from the rear. Move quietly up to the assailant from his right rear side and catch hold of his right wrist with your right hand. Quickly lift his hand up so as to bend the arm and at the same time thread your left arm through his armpit and place the palm of your left hand across the back of his right hand. Trap his right arm to your body with a clamping action of your left elbow and bend the assailant's hand down with your left hand (Fig. 111). Bearing down on his hand will bring intense pain to his wrist and, provided you can keep his arm trapped against your body, you will be able to walk him along on tip-toe to wherever you want him to go.

Fig. 111

The Sleeper

Some people, including drunks, drug addicts and the insane, are impervious to pain. Blows, locks and throws may have little effect on such people unless they are done hard enough to knock the assailant out. This is by no means easy without a lot of training.

Technique One

One method used successfully by one American police force is the *Sleeper* – a simple judo strangle applied to the point where the assailant drops unconscious. Apart from ultimately rendering the man unconscious, a strangle is usually a very frightening experience which often quietens down the most unstable of personalities. Judo fighters get used to being strangled. Occasionally they lose consciousness when submitting too late. When they come to, which does not take very long, it takes a minute or two to recover and they carry on fighting. For the uninitiated, the psychological shock takes some time to get over.

Fig. 112

Approaching your assailant from behind, whip your right arm round his throat. Bend him over backwards and kick the back of his right knee with your right foot to make him crumple. As he drops down, join your hands together and tighten your right arm all the way round the assailant's neck. His head should be at about the level of your chest and you should be pulling your own right arm in towards it. As you maintain the pressure on the neck, keep the assailant off balance backwards (Fig. 112).

As the assailant starts to go unconscious he will wheeze and gag, flail, quiver and shake, and then eventually slump. The time it takes to go unconscious is about ten seconds from the point at which the strangle is fully tightened on the neck. *Do not hold it on a moment longer.* If held on too long the strangle is lethal. Only use this type of move in emergencies: see page 31 and the caution on strangling.

Technique Two
This strangle is the same as the one shown for ground fighting (Fig. 81, page 94). It can be done equally effectively from a standing position. Approaching your assailant from behind, throw one arm round his neck so that his Adam's Apple fits in the crook of your arm. With the same arm catch hold of the bicep or forearm of your other arm and fold that arm backwards so that it slides down behind the back of his head. Apply pressure by tightening both arms. This is really a very effective strangle. It is slightly slower in application than other strangles, since the arm movements are rather complicated. Once locked in position, however, it is virtually unbreakable. When the arms are locked around the neck the assailant may try to bend forward to throw you over his shoulder or drop to the ground. Whatever he does, hang on tight, he will only hurt his neck if he moves too much. See page 31 and the caution on strangling.

Technique Three
This move is a combination of three nasty moves – a strangle, a spine-lock and a kidney squeeze. It requires a certain amount of agility and is best done on soft ground.

Approach the assailant from the front. Reach up with your right hand and pull his head forward and down. As the head goes down reinforce the push with your left hand and feed the assailant's head under your right armpit. Encircle his neck with your arm and catch your other arm to strengthen the grip. His head should now be firmly trapped under your armpit with your right arm tightening round his neck and locked to the other one.

From this position drop back to the ground and wrap both your legs round the assailant's waist. This is best done in a single move, hence the need for soft ground. As you fall to the ground make sure that his head stays trapped under your armpit. Once on the ground, apply pressure by squeezing his body between your legs (squeeze between the lower ribs and the hip bones) and lever your right arm up under his throat as you bear down on the back of his head with your armpit.

Only use this move in serious situations.

Tie strangle

This is another strangle, done from the front, which uses a common item of clothing.

Reach up to the knot of the tie and catch hold of it, inserting your fingers down behind the knot so as to touch the throat. If you imagine a punch to the throat, palm downwards, that would be the position of your hand clutching the knot.

To bring pressure on, simply turn your hand in a clockwise direction and this will tighten the tie like a tourniquet around the neck. If the tie is loose enough you could spin your whole body round, maintaining the grip on the knot.

A different grip can be used to make the same strangle. Turn your hand, palm facing up, and slide your fingers under the knot of the tie from below then turn your hand in an anti-clockwise direction to bring the pressure on.

With both of these methods the tie has to be sufficiently loose for you to grab hold of, but not so loose that twisting it has no effect on the neck.

One other way to use the tie to strangle is simply to grasp both ends of it and pull each strongly sideways so that the knot slides tight up against the neck. If this move is successful, *take care to loosen the knot immediately afterwards*, otherwise the pressure will remain on the neck, causing serious injury or death: see page 31 and the caution on strangling.

Bum's rush

The name of this move comes from the way old-time bartenders threw 'bums' out of their saloons. The essence of the move is to get the 'bum' off balance and rush him out of the door.

Technique One

Applying a come-along hold is one method of moving an assailant, although it can be tricky if there is a large weight and strength difference between you. The following move works well if you can catch the assailant by surprise. Once he is moving, and off balance, it is a very difficult move to stop.

Catch hold of the assailant by the scruff of the neck with your left hand and the seat of his trousers with your right. Tilt him slightly forward (not too much or he will fall over), and as he staggers forward (Fig. 113) keep him in that position and run him forwards and out. If necessary you can run him into a wall.

Fig. 113

Another version of this is to feed the assailant's left wrist through his legs and catch hold of it with your right. Then catch hold of his collar as before and run him forwards.

Technique Two

It may happen that the assailant is not pointing in the direction you wish to move him, in which case you may wish to rush him out backwards. To do this, sneak up behind him, whip your right arm round his neck and bend him backwards. As you do this make a half-turn to the left and half lift him on to your right hip. Support him partially on your hip, but not so much that he could take his feet off the ground, and run him backwards to wherever you want to take him, taking care to keep him bent over backwards with your arm right around his neck.

Head wrench

The head is often the key area to control in self-defence situations. A counter-punch in the face is psychologically much more upsetting than a punch elsewhere, and with the grapple techniques, control of the head often gives control of the whole body. For example, in a rough-and-tumble you can simply put your hand on the assailant's head or face and push, and this will often send him spinning to the ground.

The following move against the head can be used as a control technique or as a much more dangerous incapacitation one.

Reach up with your left hand and cup the back of the assailant's head in the palm of your hand. At the same time wrap your right hand

Fig. 114

round his jaw. Having caught the head between your two hands, twist it round in an anti-clockwise direction (Fig. 114). Keep twisting and the assailant will roll to the ground. *Great care must be exercised when doing this move*: if the head is violently wrenched in this position, the neck may break.

Apart from using the move to roll someone to the ground, it can also be used in the following situation. Sometimes a troublesome person may enter your home and sit in a chair or catch hold of something and refuse to budge. To move such people, catch hold of their head, as above and twist it. They will usually let go of whatever they are holding and you can move them on. Another way to get someone to release hold is to pinch them quickly in the upper inner thigh. If caught by surprise they will usually let go.

Irish whip

This is a straightforward control move. Seize one of your attacker's wrists with both hands. Lift his arm up slightly, dip your head under his armpit and swing your whole body through the gap (Fig. 115), keeping a tight hold on his wrist. This will bring you round behind

Fig. 115

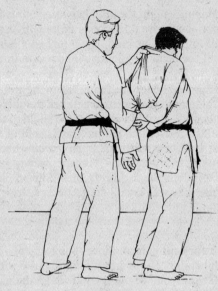

Fig. 116

him with his arm jammed up his back. Let go with your left hand and
catch his collar at the back of the neck, keeping his arm jammed up his
back (Fig. 116). You can simply control him in this position or drop
him to the ground by kicking the back of his right knee forward and
then immobilising him, as in Fig. 109 (page 136).

If you dive quickly under the assailant's armpit it is possible to
wrench his shoulder severely, especially if you do not let the arm fold
behind his back. A nimble assailant, feeling the pain in his arm, may
somersault forward to relieve it. This then turns the move into more of
a throw which you can reinforce by flipping him high in the air.

It is essential when ducking under the armpit to maintain a very
tight hold on the assailant's wrist. Your body movement will then
naturally twist his arm.

Shoulder-drop

Judo throws are fairly precise movements which require a lot of
practice to become effective. Some simple throws have already been
illustrated, such as the hip throw (Fig. 14, page 31), shoulder throw

(Fig. 62, page 75), and the back-heel hook (Fig. 15, page 31). The following throwing movements are rough-and-ready ones which can be done by the average male. They would be difficult for the weaker or small person.

If you want to lift a body high in order to dash it down, the lift used by firemen is mechanically very efficient.

Catch hold of the assailant's right wrist or sleeve and lift the arm forward and up away from his body. As you do this, crouch and step in deep between his legs with your right foot and also insert your right arm so as to catch the right leg. As you step in, spread your legs wide so as to drop your body and bring the back of your right shoulder against his front right hip at about belt level (Fig. 117). Once in position, pull strongly with your left arm so that you roll the assailant's body across your shoulders and lift him off the ground by straightening your legs (Fig. 118). Take care as you straighten your legs to keep your head up and your back as straight as possible.

Fig. 117

Once the assailant is in the air you have a choice as to how to drop him to the ground. The judo method is to wheel him across your shoulders and drop him off the left shoulder. In other words, you lift

Fig. 118

his leg end with your right hand and pull down on his head end with your left hand and tip him off the side of your body. This is best done in one continuous movement from the point at which he is first lifted off the ground.

Another way to drop him is straight back off your shoulders. If you pull him forward over your head you may hurt your neck. Whichever way you do it, make the whole movement fast so that the assailant has no time to cling to you.

Leg lift

This is another lifting throw which requires a reasonable amount of strength. In this method the assailant can be approached from the rear.

Approaching him from behind, throw your right arm round his upper body and catch hold of his clothing at about chest height. At the same time spread and bend your legs wide to the side so as to drop lower and insert your left arm between his legs and catch his right thigh with your whole arm.

Having caught the assailant with both arms as above, pull him in tightly against your body. Keeping him pinned tight, straighten your legs, keeping your back straight, and lift him off the floor (Fig. 119).

Once you have got him in the air, pull his head end forward and down with your right arm. As his head swings down and his body lies horizontal to the ground let him drop.

Fig. 119

The secret of this lift is to keep the back straight, pin the assailant to your body, and use the strength of your legs to lift him up. Do not try to lift with your arms and upper body.

Waist lift

This is another fairly crude attack which works well if you surprise the assailant from the rear or side.

As you approach from the side, duck your head under the assailant's right armpit. At the same time whip your left arm round his waist, holding tightly, and catch hold of his trousers on his right leg at about knee height. With one combined heave, straighten your legs and lift his body clear of the ground (Fig. 120). Once you have got him up you can simply drop him straight backwards, lifting strongly with your right hand as you do so. Alternatively, if you are strong enough, you can lift him right up in the air and swing him over your left shoulder to the ground behind you.

Fig. 120

The principle of the lift is the same as the previous lifts, and that is to spread the legs wide, pin the body to you, and lift with a straight back using the strength of the legs.

This move could be used against an assailant who has tried to catch you round the neck and wrestle you to the ground.

Stomach throw

This move is often seen in stage and screen fights. There are a couple of drawbacks to it as a self-defence move which can be minimised once you are aware of them. The first is that you must drop to the ground to do it: if facing more than one assailant this is not a wise move. Even if you are fighting just one assailant the move may fail, leaving you underneath on the ground. Neither is it necessarily a heavy throw. The assailant is rolled rather than dropped to the ground. Neverthe-less, it has several advantages. It is an easy throw to do and can be done by someone much smaller and lighter than the assailant. The assailant can be thrown a long way, which means that at its most theatrical the victim could use it, when backing on to a high cliff, to lob the assailant over while remaining safe himself! With practice it can be made a heavy throw and, perhaps most importantly, it can be used effectively when an assailant comes rushing straight at you.

As he moves towards you, catch hold of his upper body – either both arms, one arm and a lapel, or both lapels – and sit down as close as possible to your own feet. As you sit down, lift up a foot and place it on the assailant's stomach and kick him over your head (Fig. 121). As you push with the leg hold tight to his upper body so that he turns in the air and crashes down on his back. As soon as he hits the ground, spring to your feet. Take care that the foot you place in his stomach is firmly in the middle and does not skid off to the side, otherwise he will crash down on top of you. Also make this leg strong. If the leg has no tension in it, it may crumple as the assailant's weight comes on to it.

Fig. 121

If you can do the throw fast, especially when the assailant rushes at you, it can be a very heavy throw indeed. However you do it, take care to hold the upper body tightly until after he has crashed to the floor. This will turn him high in the air. Otherwise he will just nose-dive to the ground over your head.

Rear knockdown

Technique One

There may be occasions when you wish to aid someone else under attack. The following is a simple move which if done lightly will give you control of the assailant, or if done strongly may knock all the fight out of him.

Fig. 122

Approaching undetected from behind, grab the trousers at the back of both knees and pull strongly towards you, driving your right shoulder into his lower back at the same time (Fig. 122). This will shoot him forward and down on to his face.

Your hold can be varied considerably. Other possibilities are to insert your fingers under the bottom of the trousers or to wrap your arms round his knees. You can drive the crown of your head instead of your shoulder into the small of his back. A little experimentation on your training partner will help you to find the easiest hold to suit you.

Technique Two

In this situation an assailant is holding someone up at knife point, and you are able to approach him unawares from the rear. Since it is dangerous to the assailant's victim to knock him forward the assailant must be knocked down backwards.

Creeping up quietly behind, reach up with both hands and cup them round the assailant's eyes and pull his head violently backwards (Fig. 123). This will hurl him off balance to the floor. As he loses balance he may drop the knife. If he does not, catch hold of the knife wrist with both hands as soon as you can and wrist-twist until the knife drops.

Fig. 123

An alternative method to the above is to grasp his hair (if long enough) in one hand and kick the back of one knee forwards as you jerk him backwards.

If the assailant is about to make a downward stab at his victim, grip the knife wrist as he raises it high, wrap your other arm round his neck or grab his hair and kick his knee forward. Take care throughout all these moves not to lose sight of the knife, and wrest it from the assailant the first moment you can.

Technique Three

This move is against an assailant holding someone up with a hand-gun. Approaching quietly from behind, reach quickly over his gun-holding arm and grasp the gun, twisting it up and out to the side with a violent wrench. Keep twisting until the gun is wrested from his grasp, taking care not to point it at yourself or the assailant's victim.

As you grasp the gun, you can also kick the back of his nearest knee forwards and drop him to the ground.

Sometimes this sort of wrenching move is very effective against a hand-gun because the attacker's finger gets trapped and levered back by the trigger guard.

Technique Four

If an assailant is running away you will probably want to let him go. However, depending on the circumstances, you may wish to detain him, for which the following move is effective.

As the assailant runs away, run up close behind him and pitch him off balance to his front left corner. That is to say, not directly forwards nor directly to his left side but halfway between. To do this you will need to push with your right hand against his right rear shoulder, or in that general area, and if possible use your left hand against his left hip to push the opposite way. Alternatively, if you have the stride for it, drive your left leg beyond his left leg and in front of it so as to check forward movement, and push as before with your right hand. The leg movement in this case would be like a football tackle. If pushed correctly in mid-flight the assailant will hurtle to the ground.

For those with rugby experience, simply make a rugby tackle. Those without such experience will find the other method much easier.

Moving behind

The human body functions like a hand, which is to say it folds forwards. You can only make a fist one way, or curl up into a ball one way. Movement the other way is highly restricted. Thus the most vulnerable direction to be attacked from is behind. When dealing with an assailant it is of great advantage to be able to move behind him. Once behind you can make strangles or knockdowns, or strike the assailant in comparative safety. One Chinese Kung Fu form consists of techniques of moving behind someone. The following move is a combination of a wrestling arm-drag and Kung Fu.

Catch hold of the assailant's right wrist with your left hand. Reach up with your right hand and catch hold of his right upper arm, your hand going between the arm and body and curling round the triceps just above the elbow. Pull the arm and the assailant towards and past your right side (Fig. 124), stepping behind the assailant as he moves past you. Once you have moved behind, let go of your grip on his arm and wrist and catch him round the neck with your left arm, and apply the Sleeper or any other rear attack.

Fig. 124

Apart from the general benefit of being able to move behind an attacker, the move may be used for simply moving past someone who may be blocking your passage in a narrow corridor.

Two assailants

When facing two assailants, it is important not to spend more than a second or two on one of them. As soon as you close with one the other is sure to be moving up behind you. If you go directly for one there is always the chance that you might become bogged down. The knack when dealing with more than one assailant is to strike and then move on. For example, when faced with two assailants standing about three feet apart, instead of going straight at one, burst through the two of them as they approach, kicking or punching one as you go through, then spin round and kick or punch the other. Wherever possible try to shove one of the assailants violently into the other, cracking their heads together if possible. It is important to keep on the move and make your changes of direction unpredictable. As you move, keep punching and kicking, aiming for the highly vulnerable spots. Unless you are very quick at doing locks and throws avoid them since, if you catch hold of the assailant, he is likely to catch hold of you and slow you down.

Fig. 125

If one of the assailants manages to catch hold of you from behind and the other approaches from the front in order to hit you, your feet will have to be used to full advantage. Pretend to struggle within the embrace of the assailant behind you, and as the other comes within range lash out with your foot to his stomach or groin (Fig. 125).

If each assailant manages to catch an arm, try to throw one of them to the floor. This can be done by grasping whatever clothing you can on the assailant's body, pulling forward and at the same time sweeping back into his knee with the back of your knee and leg (Fig. 126). As he drops to the floor, get clear of his grasp and turn your attention to the other one, dealing with him as swiftly as possible. (See also Multiple assailants, page 16.)

Fig. 126

Jacket-slip

Wherever possible you must try to use whatever advantages the assailant offers you. If he has long hair, for example, then get hold of it. Often you can use the assailant's clothing to good advantage. The use of the tie for strangling has already been described. Another technique is to slip the jacket off the assailant's shoulders (thus immobilising his arms) and follow up with a punch, a kick or a throw. If the jacket is tightly buttoned up this will not be possible, but if it is partially buttoned or unbuttoned it may be.

Similarly, look to see if the assailant's trousers or shorts can be pulled down. This is a comic move but is effective in reducing the assailant's mobility. If you can pull them down, do so, then push the man over and run away.

These are obviously close-range techniques of a sort that may be useful for a woman who is being bothered by a man. She could pretend to comply, then, when close enough, quickly do one of them.

Toe tread

This technique is a fairly easy way of knocking someone over. It does not require a lot of strength or much practice. Step heavily on the assailant's right foot with your right foot, keep your weight on it, and push the assailant over backwards with your right hand clutching his throat (Fig. 127). Provided you keep your weight on his foot, he will fall over. It is not likely to be a very heavy fall, so you will have to follow up with another move or run away.

Fig. 127

Another fairly easy way to knock someone down is the karate adaptation of a judo foot-sweep. Karate men find it useful when free-fighting against someone with a wide stance.

Against an assailant's forward bent leg, swing your foot round from the side and kick the back of the knee forwards and slightly up with the top of the foot and lower part of the leg. The angle of your foot and lower leg will fit snugly behind the knee (Fig. 128). However, the whole move is one hefty kick to the back of the knee, which will send the assailant crashing to the ground without having to use the arms at all.

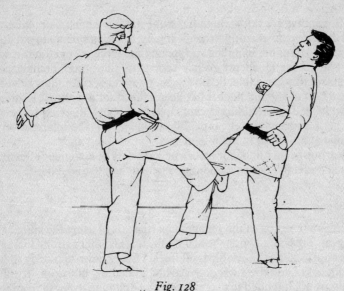

Fig. 128

Chemical weapons

Under this heading come various chemicals that may be used offensively against you and also various chemical sprays that are sold for self-defence purposes.

Various chemicals are used offensively in attacks. The list is quite long and includes such common chemicals as household bleach and ammonia. Chemicals used in these attacks may affect the eyes and respiration, or burn the skin, as do acid attacks.

All these noxious chemicals will be carried in a container, then thrown, sprayed or squirted at you. The only defence is to avoid any contact at all with the chemical. You must be especially wary of a stranger coming too close with any container, large or small, in his hand. If you suddenly find that something is being directed at you, throw up your hands and protect your face as best you can. Alertness is the only real defence in this situation.

It is possible to buy some aerosol sprays which contain some disabling agent for self-defence purposes. In Britain their use is illegal, although elsewhere that may not be so. If abroad, check whether their use is legal.

Such sprays are not without hazard. First, they must be carried so that they are conveniently to hand. It is useless for a woman to put one at the bottom of her handbag and spend thirty seconds or so rummaging around for it when violence threatens: there may not be that amount of time available. Secondly, they have to be carefully directed. In the heat of the moment it has been known for a woman victim to squirt herself and not the attacker. Even if properly directed you may still get some on yourself, especially if the attack takes place in very windy conditions or in a confined area.

Bearing this in mind, sprays can nevertheless be extremely effective if used correctly. Some cautious practice in their use is advised.

Kiai

There is a tradition in the Japanese martial arts of using the voice as a weapon. This is known as the kiai shout. It is said that a strong kiai can stun an attacker or knock birds off trees! I have known one fairly small Japanese karate expert whose voice had something of the quality of a lion's growl. It tended to overawe one and drain the strength from the legs. Go and listen to a lion at the zoo and you will perhaps understand.

The shout is used in two ways. Firstly it is roared straight at a would-be attacker to stop him in his tracks, and secondly it is used in combination with the various defence moves. For example, when used with a punch it is roared out as you make the move. This not only affects the attacker but concentrates the power in the defender's body and in the defensive move.

The shout itself must well up from the Saika tanden or lower abdomen – a couple of inches below the navel. It must be extremely loud and forceful and be an expression of one's whole body and of total fearlessness.

Searching an assailant

Most people who watch television will be familiar with police searching methods. If you need to search someone, try to get him to co-operate first. Ask him if he has any weapons and get him to hand any over. If you have to search him forcibly, get him to spread his legs and arms really wide and lean at about a 45 degree angle on a wall with his weight evenly balanced between hands and feet. Approach from his left side and place one of your feet so that if necessary you could hook the assailant's left foot away to make him collapse. Search from top to bottom, then move round to the other side and repeat. Watch carefully as you move to the other side for any signs of resistance.

When you search, do not search for any particular item. If you look for a knife you may miss a gun. The most common area for concealing weapons is the belt line, particularly the small of the back.

If a wall is not available, get the assailant to spread his legs very wide and interlock his fingers behind his head. Grasp the fingers, locking both of his hands together and make your search. Alternatively get him to kneel with his hands behind his head, grasping his hands as before.

Both with this technique of searching, and the following one of binding, there are legal complications. Searching someone may leave the searcher open to accusations of theft or indecent assault, and binding someone may constitute assault, unlawful arrest or even kidnapping. Unless a person is found committing an indictable offence, the public has no right to deprive a person of his liberty. Whereas police or security personnel may need to know such techniques, the average member of the public must use them only with caution.

Binding

Although immobilisation techniques have been illustrated, it may happen that you will want to detain an assailant more effectively and with less physical control on your part. The following technique of binding an assailant can be applied quickly and can be used as a come-along hold.

The best situation in which to apply the binding is when you have knocked the assailant to the ground and are controlling him, face down, with one arm jammed up his back (see Fig. 109, page 136). Catch the piece of rope, or whatever similar item you have handy, keep the assailant firmly pinned to the floor and loop one end of the rope twice round his wrist and make a firm knot. Stretch the other end of the rope up and around the assailant's neck then back to the same wrist, looping it again and tying a tight knot (Fig. 129). Before you tie the second knot, make sure that the arm is jammed tightly up his back and that the rope is taut between wrist and neck.

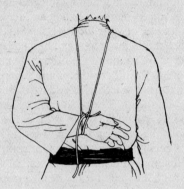

Fig. 129

The success of this binding method depends on a balance between the pain in the arm up the back and the semi-strangulation of the rope round the neck. If the assailant struggles, he increases the discomfort of either or both. For more complete control the other arm can be caught and bound in the same way, but after one arm has been secured first.

To use as a come-along hold, grasp the two strands of rope between the wrist and neck and pull. The assailant will do what you tell him and he can be escorted to wherever you want to take him. For the legal implications of binding someone, read the previous section on searching.

Dealing with martial artists

It is highly unlikely that you will have to deal with a martial artist such as a boxer or Karate-ka since most of them are well versed in disciplining themselves and their aggression. Whereas the expert is not a threat, however, the half-trained man who is out to prove himself may well be. The limitations of all these arts are that they are bound by rules and the practitioner will probably stick to them. Knowing the rules helps to deal with the man.

The first golden rule is not to fight the man at his own game. Do not box a boxer or trade kicks with a Karate-ka. Secondly, try to give the impression of complete vulnerability on your part. Act dumb and try to give the impression that you are an easy target. The aim is to get him to approach you without too much caution on his part. Thirdly, when you have to act, rush him.

Against a *boxer* try to kick in the knee, testicles or stomach. Maintain your distance. Alternatively, rush in low, dive for the legs and try to take him to the ground, where you go for joint-locks or strangles.

Against a *judo* man, punch hard to the face or stomach as he tries to take hold. Or kick to the knee, testicles or stomach. Do not let him get hold.

Against a *karate* or *Kung Fu* man, rush in fast and try to take him to the ground, where you go for joint-locks or strangles. Much karate and Kung Fu training consists of stopping kicks and punches short of the target and practising against imaginary opponents, that is to say kicking and punching in thin air. Thus their training is not very realistic. If you have to trade kicks and punches, wade in hard and fast – you may well find them paper tigers.

Against *Aikido* men, punch or kick suddenly at them. Do not leave your arm or leg in any one position long enough for them to catch it. If they do manage to catch hold, try to kick away their legs or otherwise upset their balance.

In general the strategy for dealing with martial artists is to grapple with the strikers, and strike the grapplers.

Martial artists have many advantages. They are fit, with good reflexes, used to taking a certain amount of pain, and skilled in their particular fighting movements. If you have to deal with them be very careful.

Many times the question is asked: which is the best martial art? In other words, if they fought each other, who would win? The answer is that, in the last analysis, it depends on the man. If he is rock hard, courageous, strong and fast, he will win whatever art he follows.

Women, Children and the Elderly

This chapter should not be read on its own. That is to say a woman, for example, who wishes to learn self defence, should not assume that all the advice she needs is contained in this chapter. It is essential to read the whole book, and especially the first two chapters. The self-defence situation is an open-ended one where anything can happen; therefore you must know as much about self defence as possible.

Women

The major problem for women in defending themselves is that they are considerably weaker than their potential male attackers. A figure of around 30 per cent weaker has been suggested. This, of course, is an average figure representing a spectrum of female strength and weight ranging from those women who are stronger than men to those very much weaker. Any reasonably sized woman can learn to defend herself quite effectively, and physical training can, of course, make a woman much stronger and fitter. The very small or very non-physical woman has a problem which it would be unrealistic to deny.

Given surprise, sufficient ruthlessness, cunning and a stupid attacker, any of the techniques in this book will work. However, the smaller, the nicer and more honest you are, the greater will be your self-defence problem.

When the physical odds are stacked against you in this way there must be greater recourse to your mental abilities. Awareness must be developed to the full so that trouble can be seen a mile off. Your weapons must be cunning, ruthlessness, guile and surprise. You should not feel the slightest qualm about being totally treacherous. The actual moves you make will have most effect when directed against the highly vulnerable targets such as the eyes, throat and testicles.

The self-defence situation is a very nasty one. You will experience paralysing fear and probably pain. The fear and the pain must not stop you from action. Practising the self-defence techniques in this book will get you used to a certain amount of rough handling. The real thing may well be much rougher. Do not imagine you can sail through violence unscratched, unbruised and unharmed. You will have to be a real expert for that to happen.

The main requirement is a fundamental psychological adjustment. You have to shift from a lifetime's conditioning of pleasantness and non-violence to the other end of the scale – the inhumanity of the shark. You have little chance or choice if you are weak and nice.

Women are much less likely than men to get involved in simple fights. Violence directed against women often has a specific motive, such as rape or robbery. Whereas in a simple fight men will trade kicks and blows, in motivated violence directed against a woman, the assailant will require a degree of control and is much more likely to catch hold. A woman must therefore learn the grapple defences, including ground fighting, as well as how to kick and punch.

Women must now also be wary of violence from other women. As women's role in society changes, there is a drift away from past standards of femininity. There is greater social and economic freedom plus more association with and acceptance of men's fighting values and techniques.

The Whitbread study on female aggression showed that in the three groups of women studied, over 80 per cent in each group had been in a fight at some time.

Women are traditionally believed to be particularly wild and vicious when they fight. Probably this is because they had not learned the 'rules' of fighting. However, the Whitbread study showed that punching and kicking was the commonest form of assault, followed by the more 'dirty' slapping, biting, scratching and tearing of clothes. None of these 'dirty' fighting methods requires special self-defence measures, just awareness and application of the basic moves in this book.

Robbery

Purse- or bag-snatching is a fairly common form of robbery directed against women. If the bag is snatched from your grasp and the robber runs off, there is little you can do short of giving chase. Obviously the bag must be held tightly or carried in such a way that it cannot be snatched away.

Assuming a robber has caught hold of your bag and is tugging it away, what can be done? If you are both pulling there is a good chance that the robber will spread his legs wide (front to back) as he pulls. In this case try attacks to the nearest leg such as knee kicks (Fig. 101, page 120), a sharp kick in the shin, or the *kick-sweep* (see page 159). Against this wide stance it is not difficult to upset the assailant's balance and bring him down. While you do this, create as much noise and fuss as possible, since it is not likely that the robber will want to delay too long. If you live in the sort of area where robbery of this sort is common or likely, carry your valuables on your person, and carry other items in a cheap bag which you will not mind losing.

Rape

Statistics show that rape is on the increase. Undoubtedly many rapes are not reported, and it has been suggested that reported rapes are only one-tenth of the total number.

The motive for rape is not necessarily sexual gratification. Some studies conclude that the primary motive is aggression directed against women. Such aggressors may like using force on women or humiliating them. They see women as sex-objects and categorise them as good or bad.

Many rapes are planned and are not necessarily spontaneous. A male, planning rape, may well disguise his inclinations, though signs of aggression are well worth noting.

According to a Philadelphia study, the average rapist is twenty-four years old and not obviously abnormal or even sexually odd, though he is aggressive. There is roughly a one in two chance that he is known to the victim, although this relationship may be an extremely tenuous one ranging from someone you occasionally nod to, living in the same street as yourself, to a close relative. However, any male, young or old, known or unknown, is a potential rapist.

Rapes tend to happen, like other forms of violence, during the social hours in summer rather than winter, at night rather than during the day, with Saturday night being the peak time. Roughly half the number of rapes take place out of doors. A good number of those that take place indoors are either in the rapist's or the woman's home.

In the Philadelphia study 90 per cent of all rapes were accompanied with the threat of death or the threat of a weapon. Roughness of some sort, including chokings, was very common.

To lessen the possibility of rape, a number of actions are indicated. First, special awareness is required during the social hours. When returning late, arrange to go home with another female friend. Try to wear sensible shoes and clothes and carry very little, just in case you have to move quickly. Disguise your female silhouette by wearing jeans and a baggy coat and cap of some sort. If you have to go through dark streets alone, *run* through them. Do not stop to talk to anyone. If you are being followed either on public transport, in the streets or in your car, do not necessarily head straight for home, but head for the nearest bright public place where help may be available.

A police whistle is a useful item to carry, as is a Freon horn which lets out a shrill blast – especially useful in subways where the noise bounces off the walls and is amplified. If you have to use your voice to make a noise, shout out FIRE! rather than help, and really let rip and include a few obscenities.

An experiment was made late at night in a city street in America. The word HELP! was shouted several times and there was little response. Some time later, in the same setting, the word FIRE! was shouted out and there was a much greater response. Obviously the request for 'help' requires a commitment which many people may be too frightened to offer, whereas the word 'fire' may only be a warning of something which many might want to watch or which makes them check that their own property is not in danger. Whatever you shout out must attract attention.

When getting in to your car at night, check your surroundings before you fiddle with the car keys. Before you get in, make sure there is nobody in it already. Once in, lock it so that nobody can get in from the outside should you stop temporarily at lights or elsewhere. Do not stop for hitch-hikers or for flashing lights from a car behind. It is also important not to hitchhike yourself. You will not be that much safer with another female friend or even with a male friend. Hitchhiking can be dangerous.

Since many rapes occur in either the woman's home or the rapist's, do not lightly invite a male in, or go into his house, especially if he is drunk or aggressive. Do not worry about being thought unfriendly, just be totally businesslike.

As there will be many occasions when you are at home alone you must obviously make your home secure. The front door should be strong and have a peephole and a strong chain lock. Secure all the other doors and windows. Install good lighting around the house (and garage if you have one) and switch it on before you go out for the evening. Never send your children to answer the door; always go yourself.

If you live in a block of flats, check the lift before entering and, once in, stand near the control panel so that you can press the alarm button if necessary. Avoid the use of female first names and Miss, Ms or Mrs on nameplates or in telephone directories.

When unable to avoid the company of men at high-risk times or places, totally avoid any conversation containing sexual remarks or innuendoes. Be cold, crisp and businesslike, or act dumb. Since many men cannot distinguish between friendliness and sexual come-ons, never give them the slightest opportunity to find out. Be unfriendly, even.

If threatened with a weapon such as a knife, you are best advised not to resist unless the man actually tries to use it. Make your primary objectives in the rape situation avoidance and escape. To this end, use your wits to the maximum. Act crazy or use humour to defuse the situation. Pretend compliance and suggest going somewhere more comfortable (where help may be available or there is more room for manoeuvre), hint at VD or menstruation. Use any little trick, such as going to the lavatory, to put space between you and the rapist.

If you decide to resist the rape and your various verbal strategies have failed, as I have said above, make avoidance and escape your primary objectives. If you can, stumble the man to the floor and nip out of the door. Control and incapacitation techniques are more difficult and require practice. However, the decision to resist and the choice of the method of resistance are solely yours and are conditioned by the circumstances. Nobody else can tell you what to do.

If you cannot avoid the rape starting, you have a number of options during or after it. It may not be difficult to catch hold of the rapist's testicles. If you can, squeeze hard for several seconds; this should incapacitate him. Similarly, use your teeth to take the biggest possible chunk out of him. If a lot of blood is flowing he will have to do something about that rather than about you. This also applies to enforced oral sex.

After the event, the rapist may well relax, giving you a chance to incapacitate him. One victim pretended compliance and when the rapist was dozing afterwards, broke a bottle over his head which nearly killed him through loss of blood.

After the rape you may wish to report what is a serious crime. If you do, go *immediately* to the police and police doctor. They will notice signs of distress, injury and the presence of semen, etc. You will have to answer many questions about the incident both at the police station and in court afterwards. If you delay reporting, the evidence in your favour such as distress, injuries or ripped clothing may disappear. Whether you report the incident or not, contact rape counselling services or the Samaritans. Talk over your problem; do not let it burn you up.

Children

Children may be attacked by adults, or bullied by other children. A small child can do little against an adult. Parents must take precautions such as teaching their children to beware of strangers, and not leaving them unprotected. The bigger the child gets the more chance he or she stands against older people. Even though a young child can become skilled at self defence or karate and judo movements it is doubtful whether he would be very effective against a much bigger adult. It is difficult to generalise, but it is probably not till the child gets into his teens that he starts to get strong enough to defend himself effectively.

A child does stand much more of a chance against bullies of roughly the same age. Parents who wish to protect their children against bullying should enrol them in judo, boxing or possibly karate classes. There is the problem with self-defence or karate classes that the child does not have the judgment necessary for the use of the really dangerous techniques, and could seriously injure another child. Amateur boxing is very closely supervised and there is very little chance of the child getting beaten severely around the head. Judo is probably the best basic self-defence training for children: it will make them fitter, stronger and more confident, and this alone will stop most of the bullying. As the child gets older he can combine judo with boxing, karate or self defence.

The elderly

One method of defence for elderly men has already been suggested, and that is a stout stick (see Stick techniques, page 122). Elderly women have more of a problem. However, given reasonable health and alertness there is no reason why self-defence knowledge, awareness and ability should not decrease their chances of injury from assault. Many of the techniques will be beyond the ability of a frail old lady (or man), but some may work and it depends on the vigour and alertness of the individual. For the elderly there must be a much greater reliance on precautions and awareness.

Special care must be taken not to stereotype the potential attacker. He will not necessarily be big, unshaven and ugly, but may be male or female or quite young. The mugger may be a young teenage girl, for example. Regard all who are physically able to harm you as potential attackers.

11

Self-defence Training

The techniques in this book must be learned and practised carefully. Failure to understand this may result in serious injury to yourself or your training partner.

All of the moves, especially strangles and joint-locks, must be stopped short of injury. To ensure this, agree on a submission signal, that is to say, a signal which says 'stop, no more, you've got me'. The simplest one is probably two sharp taps on the partner's body or on the floor. Tapping the body is best. When the signal is given, all action *must* stop.

The best surface to practise on is a judo or wrestling mat, since many of the moves involve a transition to the ground. If such a mat is not available, practise on something fairly soft and flat but not so soft that you cannot move easily on it. Your practice clothing should be loose enough to enable you to move easily, and strong enough to take a bit of pulling; a judo suit is ideal. Take care to remove anything metallic, such as rings, watches, necklaces, bracelets and ear-rings. These can easily gash your training partner or yourself.

The general progression in learning the moves is from solo practice, to partner practice, to free-fighting. When practising with a partner, always tell him in advance what you are going to do and make sure he understands, otherwise you will end up with a fist in your face when preparing for a fist to the stomach.

All the basic movements such as falling, rising, moving, stance and evasion can be practised alone on a mat or in front of a mirror. They are simple moves but should be made automatic through practice. Eventually, practise with a partner so that you get the distance right.

When practising the kicks and punches, start alone, making the movement slowly in the air, then gradually faster. Next, practise in front of a mirror, making combinations of punches and kicks, shadow-boxing style. After this you will need to develop some power in each move, for which a punch-bag is ideal. When you start to hit the bag hard, take care that you do not injure your hands or your feet. Wear gloves when punching and take care to keep a straight wrist. Light shoes such as plimsoles should be worn for kicking. (You are not likely to kick with bare feet in self defence.) When punching, try to stand straight with the feet about shoulder-width apart. There is a tendency to lean into the bag, bracing the feet wide. This is all right for a slugging match but not for self defence, where you have to learn to hit crisply and on the move. When punching, use your shoulders and hips to put power into the action.

After the bag, progress to practising with a partner. First of all start very slowly, an inch or two out of range. Name the move and get your partner to repeat. For example, you say, 'Hook to the face, block and counter-punch to the stomach'. He repeats and both of you move into position, but not so that either could land a blow on the other. Go through the move slowly, then faster and faster. Once you have got the feel of it, move closer to within real striking distance and start slowly again, the attacker going for light contact, and the defender with his counter-move. Gradually build up speed.

The next stage is for both of you to wear protective armour. Martial arts suppliers now have lightweight protectors for most parts of the body and this will enable you to practise the moves with full power and contact. The development of this armour has been a major advance in self-defence training. Starting slowly, build up speed and power until both attacker and defender are attacking and defending as hard as they can.

When practising those moves that contain throws, start by simply moving into the throwing position and then out again. Next take it a stage further and lift the attacker off the ground. Finally drop him to the ground, slowly at first, then gradually harder and harder. An ideal training aid is a crash-mat. This is a very thick and soft mat which easily absorbs the impact of the heaviest throws. When using the crash-mat take care not to throw the attacker on to his head or on to the back of his neck. As with the blows, name the particular move you are going to practise, get your partner to repeat, and stick to it. There is always the strong tendency to indulge in a spot of horseplay and try to catch your training partner out with another move. This is dangerous.

When practising the moves containing strangles and joint-locks, start lightly and smoothly applying pressure until the attacker submits with the two-tap signal. Gradually build up speed but *never* crack the holds on hard. The last submission stage of these moves must always be done slowly and under control.

When practising some of the weapon defences use protective armour and dummy equipment. Do not use a real knife.

Techniques with the stick can be practised in much the same progression as the kicks and punches. First of all practise solo, then in front of a mirror. Next practise on a training bag to build up power and speed. Finally practise with a partner wearing armour, but carefully, since the stick can hurt more than a blow. Alternatively, use a lightweight stick, such as a piece of medium thickness bamboo, taped or bound to reduce the possibility of splintering. This will enable you to make your practice against an armoured partner more realistic.

Having practised the moves you will be well on your way to becoming proficient. The next stage before free-fighting is to include an element of uncertainty in the attacks. Agree to a number of attack and defence moves. Select, for example, ten moves. Wear protective armour, and if possible work with two or more training partners. Get them to attack, one at a time, with any of the ten selected moves. You must then defend yourself with the appropriate defence for each attack. In this way you will learn to respond to any attack as it comes at you, whether it is with a weapon, from behind, or whatever.

Finally, extend your training into free-fighting. This is where you will learn real timing, judgment of distance and the ability to improvise. It is also good physical training.

Wear lightweight gloves that enable you to grip and punch, protective head and body armour, and light shoes. Free-fight on a judo mat using a lightweight stick and imitation knife in the following three ways:

1 *Both unarmed* Score for a good kick, punch, throw, lock or strangle.
2 *Unarmed v. weapon (knife/stick)* Score for a good kick, punch, throw, lock or strangle, plus good stab or stick blow. Also score if the weapon is knocked down or lost.
3 *Stick v. knife* Score for a good stab or cut, stick-strike and loss of weapon. Also score for any good unarmed technique.

When you free-fight, compete for the best of three points, and when applying the locks or strangles, only go for a submission, not the full thing. In this way you will discover your strengths and weaknesses and what really works. The free-fighting can be very competitive and good fun.

Fitness for self defence

Fitness is a confusing concept. Most people would probably define fitness as the ability to run a few hundred yards or climb a few flights of stairs without getting unduly puffed. However, fitness nowadays is much more narrowly defined. Fitness means having the physical (and mental) abilities that 'fit' the task. If the task requires strength then you are fit if you are strong. If the task requires strength and endurance you are fit if you have both, but not if you only have one.

A work study on American policemen showed that they required the ability to produce short bursts of high activity and strength. It was found that they needed to deal with criminals who were generally stronger than average and that they had to deal with them in a short burst of physical activity. Thus the police training programme was changed to include fifty-yard sprints and weight-training, plus increased self-defence drills. They did not end up necessarily as slim, marathon runner-type athletes – that was not the aim – but they were fit for their job.

You will acquire a certain level of fitness just by practising the techniques in this book, especially if you practise on a punch-bag and do the free-fighting. It is most improbable that you will ever indulge in a long drawn out slugging match when defending yourself. More likely, it will be a few (probably only one) bursts of high activity. Therefore, when you practise on the punch-bag, or free-fight, go hard for a few seconds, then ease off, then go hard again, and so on.

If you want to train more specifically for self defence, try *shuttle-running* and *weight-training*. When shuttle-running, mark off a 30–50 yard stretch and sprint up and down three times (six lengths in all). Rest for the same length of time, and repeat. Continue this routine over a five minute period. This can be quite hard, so the unfit should run the six lengths at an easy pace and rest longer. Gradually, over a period of time, rest less and run faster. If at all in doubt about your fitness, check with a doctor first.

When weight-training, aim first of all for an overall strength programme. The following exercises cover the main muscle groups of the body.

Legs   Put a bar with weights on your shoulders and squat up and down.

Back   Lift a bar off the floor keeping your legs straight.

Arms   Lie on a bench with the bar across your chest and push it up and down (for pushing strength). Stand bending forward at the waist, with the bar hanging down at arms length. Pull to the chest (for pulling strength).

Attach a weight to a short bar with a piece of rope and wind the weight up to the bar (for hand strength).

Stomach   Lie down hooking your feet under a fixed object and sit up and down, either with your hands behind your head or holding a weight there.

Practise these exercises in three sets of ten repetitions. That is to say, do the exercise ten times, rest for a minute or two, then repeat ten more times, rest again, then do the final set of ten. As for the weight you put on the bar, put on as much as you can handle in three sets of ten repetitions. If the weight is right the last few repetitions of the final set should be a real effort. When you can do three sets of ten repetitions, add more weight.

A weight-training session two or three times a week should be sufficient; it will probably take you a couple of months to get used to the training and start to make real strength gains.

Activities that work the heart and lungs, such as jogging and swimming, are quite good for self defence, but remember to include bursts of high activity.

There is an old oriental recipe for victory in battle. It runs: first—eyes, second—legs, third—guts, fourth—power. 'Eyes' means awareness and 'legs' means stamina. Note that awareness comes first.

BADMINTON

FRED BRUNDLE

This book provides the beginner with a basic but comprehensive coaching course, although the experienced player will also find much here to improve his game.

This book includes an account of the Laws and their interpretation, and of the equipment the player needs. The different techniques of play are thoroughly analysed with the aid of diagrams, as are tactics for both singles and doubles games. An important chapter is devoted to correcting faults and keeping fit for badminton, while a final section covers tournament play and umpiring.

TEACH YOURSELF BOOKS

JUDO

SYD HOARE

A comprehensive, fully illustrated guide to Judo which will interest and benefit all, from complete beginner to Black Belt.

This book holds a wealth of information on how traditional and modern Judo techniques are done and the best ways to achieve skill in them. Judo is presented as a sport in itself and also as a valuable training in both mental and physical development. Other topics included are self-defence, the original sources and philosophy of Judo, and advice on the preparation for contest Judo, which is the goal of all those who become involved in this martial art.

TEACH YOURSELF BOOKS

KARATE

ERIC DOMINY

Karate is the most effective form of self-defence, and one of the toughest forms of physical training possible.

This fully illustrated book by one of the founders of the London Karate Kai is designed as an introduction to Karate for the beginner. Each major school has developed its own system of Karate, so Eric Dominy covers a series of basic movements, arising from some of the Basic Postures. This forms a perfect foundation for further instruction at an approved club.

TEACH YOURSELF BOOKS

SQUASH

LESLIE HAMER AND REX BELLAMY

A top coach and a top sports writer have combined their skills to produce this book on one of the fastest growing sports in the world.

Squash is an ideal sport for the modern desk-bound city-dweller with little time for execise. This book fills the need for a comprehensive guide to the game; its past, present and future, and the strokes and tactics necessary if players at all levels are to enjoy it to the full.

This readable and lucid book covers every aspect of the game, from equipment, the rules and the various grips and shots that may be used, to match play, court language and etiquette, and general hints on fitness and practice.

TEACH YOURSELF BOOKS